BACK $EAT BILLION$

RONNY ENGELKE

Disclaimer

Although the author and publisher have made every effort to ensure that the information in this book was correct at press time, the author and publisher do not assume and hereby disclaim any liability to any party for any loss, damage, or disruption caused by errors or omissions, whether such errors or omissions result from negligence, accident, or any other cause.

Get Your Free Video Training

visit: http://www.backseatbillions.com/training

Contents

CHAPTER 1. Money

Life is wonderful, but to have an amazing life, you need to make a lot of money, and to make a lot of money, you have to start a business. A business will give you freedom to do other things like charitable activities. Family parties. Buy all the goodies you've ever wanted. A powerful person that has influence over others and to show you how easy it is for you to make as much money as you want will be an immense pleasure, because if I help you get what you want . You'll help me get what I want.

So here's a question, what do you want? If you don't know what you want, act as if you do. Do you want to make $1 million? Do you want to make $10 million? How about $1 billion. Here's what I want you to do, just imagine having $1 billion. What would you do? What would you buy? The dream home, the dream car, the dream vacation. Who would you help? Where would you go to visit? What type of restaurants, would visit? How would people treat you? Would they give you more respect?

Billions and trillions of dollars have been made from the one perfect business. What is the perfect business? It's called intellectual property. What is intellectual property? It's ideas that help people, or ideas that entertain people.   The cool thing about intellectual property is you create it once, and you get paid over and over again, residual income. Let me give you an example of intellectual property; software that runs your computer, music you listen to, movies you watch, TV shows, this very book you're reading, and it comes in many different formats . CDs, CD-ROM, DVDs, Mp4, Mp3, PDF reports, and home study courses. The business I'm talking about is selling information, and it's a huge moneymaker, because the margins are so high. This makes it the perfect business.   You can create an information product on a CD and sell it for $20-$500, depending on the information.

Lawsuits could wipe out your entire fortune, that's why it's very important to decide what business entity you want to have to protect your wealth. As you're growing your business, keep in the back of your mind that people want to sue you for almost anything.   And by having a business entity, you'll be protecting not only yourself, but also your family.   By having a business entity, no matter how small you are. It can give you a little bit of prestige, a little bit of an upper hand, because when people read about your company, they can see that you work for a real business and not some mom-and-pop operation. This way, it will make doing business easy for you.   Back to talking about protecting your company.   Always have an attorney that you can trust. Also have an attorney to do you're accounting. If you hire a regular CPA. If you get audited by the IRS. He will disclose everything to the IRS. But if you have an attorney, doing you're accounting. He won't disclose everything to the IRS, because he works for you.

Newspapers, magazines, radio, Internet, and TV. What medium will use to get your message out there so that people will buy your products? The internet can be cheap, and fast, not only to get people to buy your products, but also to test your product ideas. If you spend $300-$400, and it dies, this won't bankrupt you. TV can be huge moneymaker, but you have to know how to create commercial that will get people to ask to either buy your product or to ask for more information. If the people ask for information, you can keep following up with them, until they die or buy your product or service. Magazines are another great medium, because you can choose specific magazines and match your message to the specific person. For example, golf magazine. You can still sell products or services. Fisherman magazine. You can sell products or services about how to fish. You get the idea?

Planes, with money you can buy yourself a fancy plane. Or do you prefer a fancy car. The car of our dreams. What is it? Mercedes. Porsche. Lamborghini. Rolls- Royce. To drive you to your castle or mansion. You can have it all. Money can buy almost anything you want. People say,

"Money isn't everything" only poor people say that. Being poor doesn't make your life easier. Money does, and your family and you can also grow, because of the money you make. Can you imagine taking a family to go on a trip to Las Vegas stay at the most expensive hotel and be driven in a limousine? Take your jet, from the private airport, where your limo is waiting to take you and your family to the most amazing location. Live like a high roller, go to the most expensive restaurants, and mingle with celebrities. Money can do so much for you. Use your imagination.

Creating is a task left to God. But you also can feel like God. By changing and molding what you want out of this life. God is already inside of you. So when you create anything in this life. You are co- creating with God, it's a good feeling. For those of you that are not religious, or that don't believe in a higher power. How can you not know? Remember when you were a little kid, deep down inside. You knew, God existed. And you know, what hasn't changed. God still exists. The only thing that changed was, you grew up. Scientists don't know how protons and neutrons make an atom, and they don't know what keeps protons and neutrons together. Atoms make this world possible. One atom, combined with other atoms makes your physical world. So atoms with another atom make molecules, and molecules of the building block what, we are made of. So there is something more powerful at work here. You can't kill God.

Easy money is what you want. Get it the way you want. The way to get your commands followed by others is to learn how to influence. There is a skill you must learn from books and other successful people. You can influence people to give you whatever you want money, love ect. But you have to know what influences people. What psychology must you use to get people to buy from you, and to get people to work for you, and to use their best abilities? Here's the book, you should read called Influence by Robert Cialdini. Very powerful stuff to read ,and read that book over and over again. To see how you will apply it to your business and personal life. Remember, no matter how rich or poor, a person is. We are all made of the same genetic makeup. Everyone has a brain and nervous system ect. Not one person is different, so you can influence everyone. Influence is a skill that can make you billions of dollars.

Travel to any place, visit anywhere you want, you can stay there for months, or years. It's all up to you. Like I said Money can help you do things. I've been fortunate enough to visit many places on this earth, and I have to say. I'm grateful, because I got to see and experience firsthand how other Coulter's live. And because of that I've grown my soul. Visiting exotic places can be breathtaking, you will truly feel alive. You'll be excited about your life. Life is all about growing your soul and enjoying it as much as possible. Anytime you want to travel, all you have to do is call a travel agent and have it all booked. Don't worry about money, because you'll have an abundance in the bank. You'll know what true freedom is. Freedom is doing what you want, when you want, with whomever you want. Life is perfect. So take advantage of it.

Making your dreams come true will be easier for you to obtain because, you won't lack money. When people lack money the worse comes out in people, sending people a step back from experiencing god. When you don't lack anything your mind will be headed in the right direction. Your objection in this existence is to get closer to a higher power. Closer to the source that created you, but when you lack, your mind will be thinking about how to get that instead of how and where to grow your soul. Money is not the roots of evil. It's the attitude that a person has towards money that is the roots of all evil. If someone can kill another person for money, money didn't kill the person, it's just paper and ink, it's the other person's desire for money that kill that other person. So get it straight. Money can enhance what you are. If you are nice. You'll be nicer, if you are bad, you will get worse.

Tranquility and freedom from worry you'll have, when you have a lot of money. Money shouldn't be your motivation, money should be the byproduct of your success. Having your own business will raise your self-esteem, it has for me. Having your own business is a secret to making big money. Working for someone else is not where it's at. Now it depends what business you start that can help your life. You can start a wrong business, and it will teach you a lesson to find another business, when you have the right business. Your life will change. It will change for the good. And remember, whatever you do you're the captain of your own boat. You go, where you want to go, because now you have the freedom. Like I said, the perfect business is selling intellectual property.

Celebrities, live a life style. Everyone wants, and you can do the same. You can live like a prince or a princess. What do celebrities do? They work hard, and they play hard. They do the job once and get paid over and over again. You might not be a celebrity, and you may not want to be a celebrity, but we will learn how they get paid over and over again. We will use the same money building tactics without being a celebrity, but yet live like celebrity, have everyone look up to you, and the all the things you want, do it your way. It's that simple, later I'll tell you of a strategy to build the life you want and its simplest thing that can change your life. It's changed mine, and millions of people's lives.

Now it's your turn to live like the extravagant life, you want and desire. Have $10,000 to $1 billion in your bank account.

Satisfaction is all you want when you buy, the $50,000 Rolex, the million-dollar bracelet, not to mention feeding your ego. You can enjoy the finer things in life. And yes, I'll repeat these things over and over the get it into your brain, because it have to be in your head before you can have in real life. I want you to use your imagination. I want you to fantasize about the life you want. The more you imagine your life, the more real it becomes. You can ask my friend about what I've done? You know what I'll tell you. I've read a book, and met a very powerful CEO. But a reading in meeting these two things I've been inspired to think as if I was already a success, now. I'm thinking that I am a tycoon. I got my plates on my car that says tycoon, and on my keychain the word billionaire. Billionaire on my cell phone, the words billionaire had been written so I can focus on what I want to be. A billionaire. Billionaire's have a focus of what they want to be. Get focused.

Helping people and giving to others, not only will help you grow your soul and your wealth. But you automatically tilt the laws of the universe. You also grow. Your abilities to understand; building empathy is another important ability to grow your soul. If you give, you'll be given so much more in return. Here's an example. Look all around you. You see Edison's inventions all around you. Let me tell you a story, in the beginning of Edison's life, none of his inventions or ideas would work. But as soon as he discovered tithing giving a minimum of 10%, to his church. All of his ideas and inventions started to work. The more money, he made, the more money, he was able to give, and like I said to see Edison inventions everywhere. He gave so much that he could receive in return, much more than what he gave. And there's many more examples of people giving and tithing in secret, because they understand this law of the universe. If you don't believe try for yourself and watch your wealth grow and grow. It's normal to give 10% of what you make. Some people give more, but it doesn't matter how much you give, as long as you give to receive much more in return.

Feeling brave is what you'll feel when you make and keep a lot of money. You'll bring out the best in you. If you are unhappy with no money, you'll be unhappy with money. If your happy with no money, you'll be happier with money. Money brings out more of whom you are. So if your unhappy with no money, find a way to get happy before you get rich, because you'll enjoy life more. The way to change your feelings, is by using strategies created with an NLP, neuro-linguistic programming. The person, I recommend you learned from. Is Anthony

Robbins. The book is called "Awake The Giant Within" The reason I recommend it is because I've used the techniques. He has the good and they work. With that said, I have to give thanks to Anthony Robbins, "thank you a million!"

Attracting abundance is what you'll do. The more you have the more you'll make and the more you make the more you will share with others, not only can you help others financially, but you'll bring out the best in people. Just think how everything will be when you have your first million dollars in the bank cash, or when you make your first billion dollars. It's up to you. I've met about 400 wealthy people in my lifetime. Everywhere from executive CEO's, to celebrities. Now I say 400, because these people are millionaires have these 400 people. Seven of them are billionaire's, that's right billionaire's with a b. By watching and talking with these people. I've seen so much good stuff come out of these people. Why, because they don't worry about how they'll pay the bills. How they'll pay for the vacations. They buy what they want, when they want, whenever they wish, with whom they want. And you'll do the same.

CHAPTER 2. Perfect Business

One hundred thirty-eight dollars ($138) is all it told to make Jeff Paul $30 million-dollar fortune. Or how about $300 is all it took to make TJ Rohleder, over $100 million. How much money do you have, yes, it will take money to start your business empire, and can say it won't take $5,000 to start. And you know what, it's really up to you how much money you want to invest. Yes, if you invest more in the beginning. The bigger and quicker. Your future will grow. In the next few pages. You will discover the best way to start your business and what type of business, you will start. The business we will be talking about, of course, has to do with intellectual property, a form intellectual property. This is the only business. I know that you can start with very little and grow, potentially into $100 million to $500 million or more per year in business.

Information is the easiest fastest commodity to sell and to create. Information comes in many different formats. It can be a book, like the one your reading, it can be an audio CD, a report, a CD-ROM, a DVD video, it can be a seminar, etc. etc. like I said, and it's easy to create these types of products. Before I wrote this book. I created, a CD, 55 minutes long called Secret of Tycoon Millionaires. You can visit the web site called www.tycoonpower.com, and signup for the podcast called "Tycoon Power Show -

Business, Branding, & Profits. Now please, don't take this as if I was bragging, because I'm not. You have to understand that these products are easy to make, also another product. I created, it's a DVD called The Quick, Easy And Amazing Perfect Business. You can start to make as much money as you want to make. The information marketing business is the most amazing business to get into.

People will try to steal your money, and it's called a lawsuit. You must create the business entity to stop these people from getting none of your personal money. I have to give a disclaimer I'm not an attorney, please hire one. The best way to protect your wealth is to not have any. Now I don't mean not enjoy any. If your corporation owns the Mercedes SL500 and you use it, it's the same as if you owned it. Protect your wealth should be one of your priorities. Pick up a book on asset protection than find an attorney to make it happen for you. Can you imagine you take 20 to 50 years of your life to build your fortune here comes along? Someone that filed a lawsuit and legally takes all of your money. Don't let this happen, be prepared like I said in an earlier Chapter use business entities. Like I said, many companies. You take money from one corporation, and give it to another corporation, and then along the way you open a Limited Liability Company. You get my drift. Just hire an attorney to help you.

When was the last time you got mad at your boss and you wanted to tell him or her. How long they were for making you stay longer at work and waste your valuable time, but you knew if you said something, you could get fired. By having your company, this can happen... well, it can, but it won't be from someone in your company, because you are the boss. The only people that can fire, you are your business clients, customers and patients. You get the idea. So the only person you can get mad, that is only yourself, because you are the boss. Being the boss takes a lot of responsibility, but the job you have at XYZ Company, only gives you a little responsibility. Or a lot. Nonetheless, you weren't compensated for your available time. By being the boss. You'll find yourself making more money and feeling more fulfilled in your career. Just because you are the boss doesn't mean you can waste time, you must manage it wisely. It's one of the most important asset, you have.

State and county all have rules to follow, when you start a business. Make sure you get all the appropriate licenses to operate your business, and if you need special licenses from the government. You must be wise on does permits. As before, like I recommended to get an attorney to help. The county you do business in will give you any fines they can possibly give you, why? Because this is another source of income to the state or county. It's a racket, but you have to

13

fallow the rules to play in the business game, and you must be on top of these rules and regulations. Especially when you start to make the money. Always be ethical in your business dealings, but find legal ways to protect and save your money. The government will take a large part of its through taxes.

Deposit all your checks, cash and credit card slips into your business checking account. It's very important to manager money. Keep it in the bank. It's no fun to have 100,000 Cash and lose it. Nowadays, all you need is a credit card. Can you imagine, if you had to send $50,000 cash to accompany you do business with. It's much easier and safer to write a check or have the money electronically transferred. It's very important. You balance the account. You must know where every dollar goals, and you must know where every dollar comes from. Respect and money, because if you don't, you can easily lose it. Keep track of your personal money. If you start the corporation. You will give yourself, a paycheck, and of course bonuses, because you are the boss, but never just take money, because then it's considered stealing. So if you want extra money, just have a corporate meeting and give yourself a bonus, alone or a grant.

Fast business grows is what you want, the fastest way to have a product is the license it from someone else. And also license the marketing pieces to help you sell the product you get. Once you acquire the licenses, you can just start to advertise off-line or online and start collecting cash. For example, I was searching online, and I found the product called information marketing boot camp, it sells for $397 and four additional $400. I was able to buy the reprint rights world to free to the product and the most important marketing pieces. By licensing someone else's product, you save time and headaches and also you don't waste money testing to see what products people want to buy. Licensing is a shortcut method to get a product. The next best way is to get the resale rights to a product. Most resale rights state that you get a percentage of the price anywhere between 25 to 50% of the retail price. This is the next best thing to do to get into business. Eventually, you want create your own products.

Impulsive buying is what you want to take advantage of the make big money and to get big profits, you must accept credit cards. They don't have a merchant account you aren't in business. Let's say you want to sell the $5,000 seminar, not every person has $1000 cash. So they will use their credit card to buy your products and services. Another example of product was sell information marketing boot camp. It sells for $397. Not everyone will buy that with cash, so they'll use the credit card. If I wasn't able to accept credit cards. I would lose a lot of money. Think about, when you want an expensive item, how do you pay for? Exactly with your credit card, or some type of other credit. Be smart accept all major credit cards. Don't worry about the fees. If you have a computer. You can search for merchant account services online using google.com, or you can use paypal.com to collect money for you.

Margins are very high in the information marketing business. This business is also easy to do. Once you create your product, or license your product, you'll get paid over and over again, residual income. This gives you the time to make other projects. Basically adding more streams of income each time you create another product. This business will give you the lifestyle you want. Information selling can make you millions of dollars. Just like the other people I talk about on the previous pages. You can sell information almost about any subject. It doesn't have to be about making money. They can be about shooting a better golf game, or can be on how to train your dog or cat or horse. The subjects are endless. So create products you enjoy. A side note, make sure you sell subjects that people want to buy.

Risk is something you want to keep to a minimum. The safest type of marketing to use is direct response marketing. Why? Because it's safe, and will give you the results you need. Image marketing doesn't work, and if it does it take a long time. And a lot of money to make it work. So what you really want is to know how much is each dollar spent on advertising, will it bring back, if you spend a dollar in the get back $.10. You will want to improve. That number, if you spend one dollar and bring back two dollars. Then I would sell everything at home, to put into the business and make a bundle, and the only way to do that is to get good results. Track your advertising to make it better. Always be testing, your marketing ideas, because you never know when you spend one dollar. It might bring back $100. You can test your sells letter. You can test your telephone scripts. You can test your commercial on TV or on the radio. With the Internet, you can test many variables cheaply.

Copywriting is the most important job. The job of writing a sells letter that will get the money. Large amounts of money. Anyone can write a letter, but not everyone can write a letter that will cause a person to go to their pockets to pull out money to give you for your product. But how do you learn how to write a sells letter. The way to learn, is to practice. Every piece of sells letter you receive in the mail or online copy it in longhand for your brain will pick up the strategies of writing a persuasive letter to get the money. Please don't be confused with manipulation. Manipulation is bad, but persuading is good. Manipulating his when only you win, when the person does what you want. But persuasion is when you win, and the other person wins too. If you aren't tight budget. I recommend that you go online and seeing what products you want to sell, and save web page on your computer, print them out, and start writing them by hand. Only save the web sites that cause you to want to spend your money.

Results are what you want, when you spend money on advertising. That's why I'm going to talk about the cheap guaranteed way to get results. The two types of advertising are: the one-step. this type of advertising is where the ad is asking for money. The other type of advertising is called 2-step. The two-step ad is when a person reading the ad inquires about getting more information, they can write you, or give their name and mailing address over the a 1-800 phone number and listen to a recorded message. You can send the free report and the report will always be the sales letter. The amazing thing about the two-step is, let's say, for example. You are thinking about making a product for horse owners, how to stable a horse for free, that's the product you are thinking about making, but you want to test to see if people want to learn how to stable a horse for free. So you place, a small, classified ad one inch by two inches to offer a free report. How to stable a horse for free. Call 24-hour recorded message 1-800- horse. If no one calls. You just saved yourself a bunch of money and time. Some people create the product first and then decide to sell it, come to find out nobody wants it.

More people will call a one 800 recorded

message, because it's nonthreatening. As you read in the example before. You asked the person to call a free recorded 24hour message. People think if they have to call and talk to a live representative. The person calling doesn't want to get sold, so that's why you use and one 800 voicemail system to capture the persons name and mailing address. Nowadays, you ask for the e-mail also. Once you get the person's name and address or e-mail, you can test different sells letters and sell different products. Get a magazine and read some of the ads, pay attention to the ads that grab your attention, and see if they have a free 24-hour recorded message. Read magazines on the subject you like, and if you see an ad that grabs your attention, and it has a one 800 voicemail, act like the prospect and call. Give your name and address and see what that company does to get clients, and try to think like a marketer. You can also send people to a web page, and collect their info, than send them to the sales page.

Fulfillment can be handled by fulfillment centers. The center can send orders, they can mail the sells letters, so that you can have the free time to do business. To work on your business instead of in your business. To grow your business and the good part of it is you don't have to worry about employees, hiring, firing, politics, and taxes, etc. etc. outsourcing as a great tool to use in your business. Not only will it help you in business, let's say that company you hired is not doing business the way you like, well. You can fire them and not have to worry about a lawsuit. But outsourcing, you have the option of getting companies to compete for your business. The thing. I outsourced or handling the voicemail leads, customer service, almost all of my office functions. The only thing I don't outsourced is managing the money and the sales copy. It is written to sell my products. Never outsourced those things. The only way I would outsourced the marketing is, if I know they are great copywriters.

Write everything down. You must do for the following day, and put them in order of importance. Always keep a to do list, to stay organized. But the list keeps you on track of all the things that have to be done to make money. I know lots of business people that have a very large to-do list, and you'll notice people that write the things down, tend to be more successful, so you should write down what you must do. Theirs plenty of organizers on the market, but you know what all you really need is a pen, and a paper. Nothing fancy, unless you want it. The secret, I learned when I wanted to make large amounts of money, not only did I do it in my personal life, but also in my business life. We'll talk about goals on another section, but just keep in mind to write down the things that have to get done, and watch. You will be more successful.

CHAPTER 3. Growing

Twelve hundred percent. How much do you want to grow in one month, in one near? 500%, or is it 5000%, or more. Every entrepreneur has different ambition. And that's OK. If you want to grow less. That's OK as long the as you're doing your own thing. My ambition is to have $1 billion net worth in 20 years or less. If you have an ambition to make $1 million a year, or $200,000 a year. That's OK too. But to make $200,000 a year. You need to think about how to grow your business, and there's only three ways. The first way, bring more customers in. The second way sell larger quantities to customers. The third way sell more often to the customers. These are the only three things to bring in more money. Here's an example. If you're selling $200,000 a year, and it takes a thousand customers to make that money and each spend $200. Just find their way to increase everything by 10%. So now its $220 1100 people, but now you generate $242,000 per year. So always be on the lookout to increase these three processes to increase revenue, and you don't need large percentages of increases to make a huge amount of difference.

The more that you reinvest your profits back into your business, the faster and better your company will be. But here's what I'm talking about. Taking $138 and turning it into $50 million Empire. The only way to do that is to reinvest your profits. You know it's not necessary to reinvest all the money. If you make $10,000 a month. You must reinvest at least 50%. After some time, when you're making $200,000 a month. You don't have to reinvest $100,000, it would only take $50,000. But of course, it depends what business you get into. I'm pretty sure you know that these numbers referred to the information marketing business. Can you imagine making $200,000 or more a month? Now remember this, this is not profits. This is revenue let's say you get to keep 50% as your money. So if you increase your revenue. You increase your profits just keep down the expenses.

The more money you want to make, the more time it will take. So in the beginning, you outsource most skills, and when you start to grow, your higher part-time employees. than full-time employees, but it all depends on how much money you want to make, the more money you want to make, the more people and outsource companies it will take. Don't think that for one minute, you can make massive amounts of money on your own. If you want to make a $1 billion dollars a year. It's going to take a bunch of people to help you. It is said that for every $1 million, a millionaire has, he or she has employed 10 people, so if you want to make $1 billion. It will probably take about 10,000 people to help you, where you outsourced it, or you hire employees or a combination. All of this is up to you. What industry will you choose? How much money do you want to make? These two questions will determine how much money you make.

Invest your surplus cash into different business opportunities. You can bankroll a new company and own part of the equity, and let someone else run that company, or you can invest the money into tax-free municipal bonds, or you can invest in zero-coupon bonds. Let's talk about zero-coupon bonds. Everything I'm talking about here, you will have to talk to a stockbroker. When you call a stockbroker. Tell him you want zero-coupon bonds that mature at least 10 years or more if you want 20 years the cheaper. It is. So if you want a $5,000 zero-coupon that matures in 10 years. You will pay more than 20% of the value on. If you wanted to wait 20 years it will cost a fraction of the maturity face value. The other thing to invest your surplus is tax-free municipal bonds, even though it says tax-free. It will be tax-free while it's maturing, but as soon as your cash it in, you'll have to pay taxes. And like I said, just call up any broker, ask him or her some simple questions.

Profits is what you're looking for, along with growing your profits, safely growing your money, it is very important that you analyze all business endeavors. Because if you get into the wrong business, you could lose a bundle. What I recommend is networking with other business people, and finding out what they are doing to choose a business. Now that I'm talking about is of course investing your surplus. Also , you can look to invest your money outside the United States, but just keep in mind the money exchange rates. If you where to do business in England. You would pay $1.67 per 1 British pound. So can you imagine, you invest your American dollar and a few years' cash out in exchange for American dollars? So if you are able to grow your money into a hundred thousand pounds. You can exchange it for $167,000 dollars. Like I said before, lookout for opportunities to grow your money.

Easy money is what you want, and the best way I know, how is to niche your business. For example, your business must be directed to a specific group of people. Not everyone is your customer, so if you can target your products for a specific group. Like selling only to dentists, and not to doctors. You can specifically create a product that will generate large profits. Example, time management, to make it general, time management. You could probably ask for $15. Maybe $29, but not more than $50, but if you make it specifically for group of people fo example, time management for the dentists. You can charge $200-$500. Even if it's the group of 50,000 people. You can still extract millions of dollars from that market. There's plenty of business niches, you can choose. It's really up to you. The best way is to go to the S. R. D. S., I'll explain what S. R. P. S. is and how to take advantage of it.

Master rights to your products will make you the most money. Master rights just basically is, the ability to sell others reprints or resell rights to them for a large amount of money. Here's an example. If you create private sells for $500. And of course you own the master rights to it, you can sell the reprint rights for $1997-$5,000. It all depends what type of product. It is, or you can sell the resell rights. And you keep 50% of the money. If you buy reprint rights from someone else in the beginning of your business. That's perfect the way to go before you create your own products. Of course, you want, royalty free rights, so that you make the most amount money. If you buy those resell rights and have to pay 50%. That's OK to, you won't make as much money. You know, that's how I got started. In my business, and then eventually, I create my own products.

Time and money go hand in hand. If you want to make one million in profits. How much time will it take for you? If you don't have any experience in business , or you're not a high million dollars , earning executive, then the next best thing to do is to start your own business, but not just any business, of course ,I'm talking about the information marketing business. You know , in this business it doesn't take a lot of money to start, not like a franchise where you have to pay between $70,000-$250,000 just to open, and here's the problem by buying a franchise . You just basically bought a 50 to 90 hour or more a job, and I can speak from experience the information business will give you freedom to enjoy your life. If you have read this far. I hope you're getting excited about finally changing your life for the good, and leaving the 9 to 5 rat race, and begin to make real money, real fast.

Sales is what you want, and the only way to sale more is to have credibility. When people believe you, then you'll sell more. When you sell more, your profit more there's ways to build credibility with people. First, you must have confident and dress successful. You can get other people to talk about and your accomplishments. You can give yourself a business title, for example, I am the founder and CEO of Nosrak Corporation, and people will treat you different when they know you are, the CEO of something. I know of one individual that has a Ph D. at the end of his name so people call him Dr. what you know, and what I. We both think Dr. as a medical doctor. What he did was to send away for a home study course on how to be the preacher, and he was given the title of Ph D. as a minister. Another way to build credibility is to write a book. When you hand your book to someone to look at, they look at you in a new way. Another way to build credibility and livability is to do what PR campaign, getting newspapers to write about you getting interviewed on the radio, getting interviewed on TV, writing articles for magazines. Just get your name out to the media. Be seen with famous people, and pictured with famous people.

Most media, like TV, radio, Internet, letters etc. all can deliver the marketing message quick. Some media faster than others, but what you must do to harness and to extract the most money is to study the medium Remember it's all about the customer, what are their buying habits, can you profit from their habits. You got ask yourself those questions to make large amounts of money, because if you aren't careful. You can lose a lot of money. You know, if you send the wrong marketing message to the wrong medium, and it's the wrong people, you'll lose your money. Even though you were smart to test with little money. Still, you don't want to lose money. Always know, what your market is. The people that buy what you have for sale. I learned that I want to catch fish in a barrel. Not in the big ocean. Basically. There's three things to think about; have the right message, use the correct medium that gets the message to the ,correct people.

Know how to market your products, study other businesses. Invest in home study courses on how to bring in customers, to make more money, and to sustain growth. No matter what business, you get into. It's all about the marketing. If you're a consultant. You should be a marketer first, and a consultant second. Because if no one knows about what you have to offer, than no one will buy what you have. If you want more information on how to double even triple your profits and bring in more customer's clients and patients in one-month than all year long, visit this web site www.tycoonpower.com and click on the training tab. Remember your a marketer first, and consultant, Dr., agent, electronic store owner, etc. etc. second.

Credit cards can be a wait to bankroll your business. But if you don't have any credit cards. Then you can ask your friends and family for the money, and if that doesn't work out, get a second or third job. Cut back on money you spend. Another great idea is to use the crowd funding sites such as kickstarter.com, and indiegogo.com visit both to see which one works for you better. Or another idea you can do is create a sales letter, and put it up on the web, sale the product than once it sells, than create it. I did that once with one of my info product. I put up a web site with the sales letter, (this is for an information product) had the outline of the product done. Once I sold one product for $2,000 than I sat down to create it.

Skills, you can get from a partnership. Money, you can also get from a partnership, just make sure you can get something from a partnership.

If you have a friend and he doesn't have skills, money, or something to offer, then don't become partners. Just because your friends. Yes, it would be nice, but if you're ambitions and he or she is lazy. Then you'll have problems. When you start a partnership, you have to be very careful, because whatever your partner does will affect you. If your partner borrows money on the business name. And it's behind your back, and if the money isn't paid back. You are responsible for paying back the money, even though you didn't sign your name to the paperwork. So I don't recommend a regular partnership. I do recommend a limited liability partnership. I have to give my disclaimer I'm not an attorney if you need an attorney get one.

How to set yourself apart to guarantee you, the large part of the market. The way to do with this is to have a unique selling proposition (USP). Something that sets you apart from the competition. For example, many years ago, Domino's pizza was using this USP hot fresh pizza in 30 minutes or less or it's free, they took so much business away from the big well-established, Pizza Hut. The way to have a unique selling proposition is to get a few pieces of paper. On the first piece of paper write these words; you know how..... Of course, what follows next is the problem, you solve. On the next piece of paper. Write; what I do is..... And begin to write what you do to solve the problem. Here are example on the first piece of paper answer that question in, do you know how example, you want to have hot pizza, but it takes forever to get it..... What I do is deliver hot fresh pizza in 30 minutes or less, or it's free. You get the idea. You can have your own USP on guarantee, service, quality, but never do it on price, because if you live by price. You'll die by price.

Respect is what you'll get when you give a speech (public speaking.) People will give you credibility, and you'll be able to influence people from the stage. And you can make a lot of money selling your products at the back of the room. If you are afraid of speaking, that's OK. It's normal to be nervous, no matter how many times I get on stage butterflies always come into my stomach, Might, start to sweat. Because I know, I want to do a good job, but as soon as I stepped on stage my fear goes away. So my answer to you is just do with, you will always be nervous that's OK. If you're worried about sounding dumb, don't worry, it's everyone laughs you laugh to, and have a great time. If you've never given a speech. If you want some experienced speaking. I recommend you join Toastmasters, you can go online, type in Toastmasters on a search engine, and find in join the club in your area, it's a friendly place that allows you to actually speak in front a group of people, that speeches range from 5 to 20 minutes, even with five minute speech you will feel the psychological impact of overcoming your fear.

CHAPTER 4 Strategies

You can't save time, you either use time or lose it. The only thing you can do is manage what you do. If you want to start a business, but you say, I don't have any time. That's a sign that you are too busy working to get rich. So what I have to tell you is start your business part-time. To make time for your business empire. Watch less or no TV at all, sleep less, do whatever you must do. Manage your activities. Like I said before, write a to-do list. Once you do all the activities of business, it's time to schedule time to learn more about business strategies, and selling processes. And because if you want to sell a $5,000 product. It takes specific psychological strategies to get people to spend $5,000, and it takes another strategy to sell a $100 product. Manage your activities right, always learn and always grow.

Competition will be educating themselves to finding new and better methods to do business, and take away business from you and your profits. The solution to do this is. You should have a budget every year to buy books, home study courses, go to seminars, and hire consultants Always be expanding your mind. I used the slight edge principle, every year I have a budget of $10,000. And it's been growing. I attend seminars, buy home study courses, listen to other speakers, even though I have a lot of knowledge. I educate myself and pay attention , because if one person , or one book says something in away and it clicks in my mind, then I am having better results, because the slight edge principle is that work. Imagine you listen to someone who what they teach you how to save $250,000. Saving this money is the same as making this money. Always be investing in your education and expanding your mind. Once you expand your mind, it will never go back to its original size.

Give 10% of what you make and watch what happens to your income, your fortuen will automatically tilts the laws of the universe in your favor, yes , I know I spoke about this and other previous chapter. But this is an important principle to do, and to understand. If you give, than you shall receive, it's that simple. Once you give just pay attention to see what opportunities come into your life. But not only will you be blessed with money, but other good fortunes, other worldly things. But here's one thing to keep in mind when you give, give with good intentions, not with selfish intentions. You'll feel perfect knowing you have helped other souls get through their journey called life. Read the books that talk about tithing. Give 10% or more, and watch what happens just believe, and do it now.

Foods you eat affect your health. You must have a healthy diet. Watch what you eat. Have checkups, once a year. If you're getting older than look into HGH (human growth hormone) I must give my disclaimer not doctor if you need a doctor. Please hire one. As you have reached 25 years of age, your body produces less human growth hormone. The substance that helps keep us young, and you get older. Your body produces less. The way to combat the body natural deterioration process is to eat healthy, work out with weights, and take human growth supplements. Also vitamins to replenish your body, remember what you've heard, you are what you eat. Every seven years you have a completely new body, so it's vital to feed your body. The proper nutrition to build new cells, and to regenerate. Eat less bread, eat more fruits, vegetables, Drinkwater, and no sodas. Basically eat less sugar.

Ideas are everywhere and to get a best ideas for your business is to hire consultants. They can save you so much time and money and make you a ton of cash too. Consultants are outside looking in. When people are outside looking in, they can have better ideas of what needs to be done to grow. It's like when you watch people playing chess or checkers. You can see what the best moves to make to win are. Well, it's the same when you hire consultants. You will need all kinds of consultants. If you want to grow your business. There are two consultants. I recommend, and they are Kevin Nations, and myself. These two wonderful and intelligent people can help you grow your business 10 to 20 times over what you are now. And yes they are expensive. If these guys can help you make 10 million, hundred million dollars, then they are cheap. Use every type of consultant to grow your business.

Other industries can give you better ideas and strategies to grow your business. Aside of hiring consultants, you can also look at your competition to see what they are doing. You also can see what a company is doing in another industry, see if you can adapt those ideas and put it to use in your company. Keep an open mind to new ideas and strategies because you never know where the idea or strategy will come from that can make you an extra $2 million to $200 million. You always want to be growing and taking a large part of the market , and once you have a large market penetration do everything you can to extract the most, money , because if you don't someone else will . Another way is to meditate. Always keep a pad of paper and a pen to write down your ideas, or something you saw that will help you grow your business.

Focused on vision, you want. So that you will get the results you want for growth. The mind is the mysterious thing. And scientists are still learning how it works. Here's a strategy that will help you. Whatever you think about the most will happen in your life. If you think about not going bankrupt, and that's what you'll get. If you think about making $10 million a year, and that's what will happen. The way to use this strategy is to use the affirmations in the present tense for example. I make $1 million a year. You have to have feelings, and really see yourself accomplishing this goal, and also write down the affirmations for example. I enjoy making $100 million per year. Think about it three times of day. When you wake up in the morning. In the afternoon, and before you go to sleep. Don't worry about how to make $100 million per year. Your mind will attract the right people situations and resources.

Success is an attitude. If you don't know how to do something, act as if you do. You will act as if you are in the knowing of what to do. Control how you feel, like I said, act as if you know, and you'll be surprised when you get it done. It's another vital ingredient for success. Practice this tactic every day, and you'll get better and better at it. You'll see what I mean, this strategy. I picked up from Marshall Silber. He authored the book "Passion Profit and Power." I recommend you get this book in your personal library. Read and act as if you know, how to do, what needs to be done. Many successful people have used this strategy to a mass vast amounts of wealth money and power. Don't let anyone take you down, on how you think because you are what you think you are.

Profits can also grow if you reinvest the money coming in. it's very important to keep overhead to a minimum. Always know where the money is going. All expenses, and see if you can cut back 10% in each category. Then after sometime cut another 10% in each category is what you can do try to buy in bulk. Try to pay up front, companies will discount your payment by 2% to 5%. If you paid early. If you are paying too much for insurance. Look for another company to give you a quote. Always be asking for quotes of at least three to five companies. You buy from. This strategy can save you a ton of money per year. I was able to save $178,709.73. By applying these techniques.

File the correct business paperwork with your state, county, or government. To help you in monitor this process, retained an attorney. An attorney, not only can file papers, but can help you protect your wealth from being taken because of a lawsuit. Pay an attorney, a monthly retainer fee. Even if you don't use the attorney, because if you need him or her at a moment's notice they are there. Attorneys can also help sue other companies or people, if you're doing a leveraged buyout. You'll need a few attorneys and not any attorney, but an attorney. You can trust. The best way to find a good attorney is to talk to other people, watch TV specials like trials on TV. It's a vital to have an attorney that can touch people's feelings because people make decisions with feelings first and back it up with logic. So if you can find an attorney that can change the jury's mind. With feelings and give them away to think logically. You have a winner.

People have money to spend, so you have to learn about selling. You can learn how to sell from books, home study courses, or other salespeople. The book, you should read is called influence by Robert Cialdinni. Another person. You can learn from it is, Kevin Nations, he is the creator of R.A.P.I.D. Selling. Kevin has a home study course. You can visit his web site by going to www.KevinNations.com. Just to let you know, I don't make any money from referring you to him. My only concern is that you succeed, and I don't have all the resources to help you. But I know where to get it. The reason I recommend these things, because I bought these two products and it's tremendous, how much you'll learn and make. Once you apply the specific tactics. You'll want to learn from people that have done it, or people that are doing what you want to learn.

Small amounts of money can be raised by selling your corporate shares. You can do what's called an intrastate placement. Where the people you sell shares to live in the state were your corporation resides. Or you can do what's called a private placement. This tactic will help you save time and money, because to do what's called on initial public offering will cost a ton of money, and it will take lots of time. If you do any of the above strategies. You will save $40,000 on the Registry of your shares, the SEC. Before I continue a have to give my disclaimer and not an attorney if you need one get one. If you want to raise $300,000-$5 million. This is the strategy, you can look at, to implement. The only drawback is that you'll be giving part of your company away. Just keep in mind that you must control most of the shares.

Shortcut strategies is what you should be looking for all the time. Here's an instant wealth builde you can do. It's called reverse merger. You do reverse merger, instead of an IPO an IPO takes lots of time and money. But to save time, you do a reverse merger. This technique was used by Anthony Robbins to create $400 million in one-day. What you do, by a company that has done business in the past. They already done an IPO, and has been traded publicly. You will be buying what's called a shell company that doesn't do business anymore, and doesn't happen to have negative marks or positive marks. Let me explain what this story. Anthony Robbins bought a pharmaceutical company that wasn't doing business anymore. The shares were trading at fourteen cents ($.14). Anthony Robbins was able to buy 95% of the shares and in one-day each share was worth about $15. If you need help doing this type of transaction go to google.com and type in reverse mergers. The only drawback is. You need to have some money in the bank. Depending on which stock exchange you want to concentrate on. The minimum is $300,000 or more, but you save time.

Leveraged buyout, is a great tool to use. What is a LBO, it's financing and the company's buyout with the companies owned assets. Billions of dollars have been made. Using this tactic. this idea can also be used in a smaller scale. Let's say you want to buy a company for $1 million, and the company was on a property worth $500,000. You can borrow 80% of the value and if you have equipment worth $200,000. You can borrow 50% of the value of the equipment, and if you have accounts receivables. You can sell these for 95% to 98% of the value. If there's any debt, you can discount the price by the amount of debt and take over the debt. With all the borrowing, and with the business owned cash flow. You can buy the company. The thing to keep in mind is, you'll have to carefully analyze how much money will come in, to pay for the monthly debt payments. So with our example, you would have $1 million. Most importantly know, you need attorneys, accountants and consultants to help you to make this transaction.

Cut taxes is what you must keep in mind. The

more taxes you save, the more money you can keep. The more money you can keep, the more you can invest. Yes, only pay the minimum amount of taxes. Can look into setting up an offshore account to pay less taxes. If you need information please contact, a specialist. Now what I mean is to transfer your corporate entity, only the paperwork and not a facility. You'll save a bundle of money. The USA government says that corporations will save trillions of dollars on taxes. Always be on top of the latest tax laws, because they the government can put you away, just like Al Capone. Your best bet is to hire an attorney and not a CPA. A CPA works for you, but when the IRS asks him any questions. He works for the IRS, but if you hire an attorney, he truly works for you, and when the IRS as asks him any questions about your business. He won't answer them.

CHAPTER 5. You

Write down why you want to succeed. Always review your goals. Always keep the big picture in your mind of what you want to accomplish. The way to stay motivated is to think of what you'll get when you finish your goal. For example. $1 million. Think of what you can do with that money. Have a fantasy session with your private thoughts. Another example, how will you feel when you lose 30 to 40 pounds of ugly fat? How will people treat you? Will they treat you good or bad? You'll feel excellent. Just write down how you'll feel and this will keep you motivated. Imagine the picture of what you want. Write down how you would feel by accomplishing your goal. I know you will feel incredible. When you make your first $10 million. Imagine everything you'll buy and do. When you write, use present tense words and vivid words. For example, the car I drive is a Phantom Rolls-Royce, and it's a burgundy color. I owned a 12 thousand square-foot home in Las Vegas Nevada. Keep writing why you want your goals, and something amazing will happen. Your wishes will come true.

Map your way to your destination. A ship without a rudder is lost. The same applies to you. No where you want to go first. Before you set your actions. Because if you don't know your destination, then you'll be in a place you don't want to go. Write down what you want, I know I'm repeating myself, but you must understand and know, what you want, and your mind will make it happen. Don't be concerned with how. A story told by Anthony Robbins, he says. A lady was told to think of how much money she wanted to make in 12 months, and she said. $100,000. She just kept thinking about it and in the 12 months. She made $100,000, and not knowing how she would make that kind of money. The next year she was asked the same question and the answer was $250,000. And on the 12-month she made the $250,000. Without knowing how to make that kind of money. The first hundred thousand dollars. She made by buying a lottery ticket. The $250,000. She made the same way. This story illustrates that your mind will attract, whatever you think about the most will come true.

Track what you've done. Make a list. This is important, but the most important ingredient is to take action. Do something, even if you're scared, because you'll learn what needs to be done. Everything that's been accomplish came from action. If you have a tremendous knowledge, and don't do anything, then what's the use? Help people, humanity. Common sense is not as common as you think. So if you know something, teach it to others. Take action. Action is better than feeling hopeless. Remember only looking to change your life. So take action. Action. Action. Here is a secret, the biggest secret...Is to take action. If you want to lose 40 pounds take action. If you want to quit your job, take action. If you want to start your business, take action. If you want to make $1 billion, take massive action.

Time is the most valuable asset, use it wisely. Profits and results is what you want.   Stay focused. If you've started special diet, and then stick to it.   Don't change to another type of special diet.   If you started a direct response business. Keep with the period don't try to start a theater business. Keep focused. Do one project at a time, too many things will where you out, and then you will accomplish nothing. Focused on what you want. Focus on the big picture. My big picture for you is to be successful in business. I want you to focus on losing weight, and having better relationships, this is too many things to think about. Only focus on one thing at a time. Look at Donald Trump. He specializes in real estate, and his empire has grown into billions of dollars.   Yes, he's into casinos, but those casinos are not successful. As his other real estate businesses. Focus on one project, one business at a time.

Thinking positive won't guarantee success, but thinking negative will guarantee failure. Thinking positive is the big rule to keep in mind. Thinking positive can be the one thing to make you successful and negative thinking can be your failure.   The mind is an amazing instrument.

Scientists are still learning about how your mind operates, and they say, that the mind is not in the brain... how mysterious. So keep in mind that thinking positive won't guarantee success, but thinking negative will guarantee failure. The same goes for people you hang out with. If they are negative, don't be with them. If you watched too much bad news on TV, turn it off. If you listen to the negative music turn it off. Any negative activity should be blocked from your valuable life. Just do it.

Two-step marketing, voicemail follow-up, they should be part of your marketing plan. Along with publicity. Publicity is a powerful tool to use. It can make you millions of dollars. Study on how to get publicity at the end of this book. You can get information on publicity in the resource section. What is two step advertising, this is when people call you for more information from your advertising. For example , complacent and magazine "protect your wealth from the IRS, get your free report, call 1-800-save -money, 24 hours free recorded message". This and gets people to call and ask for information. You collect their names and address. Now you can send themselves letters, after sells letters until they buy or die or asked to be taken off your lists. That's called follow-up on your leads. Following up on your leads can make you rich. It said that you have to make between seven and contacts for a person to buy. You can Also do this on the internet. Offer a free report for the person's email, and follow up with emails.

Market to a group of people that want to buy what you have to sell. The average person's thinking is like this, he or she thinks of the invention and spend a lot of money and a lot of time to make the invention, come to find out, no matter how wonderful the invention is, no one wants to buy it. So we have to think backwards. We first find a group of people that want to buy, what we might want to sell. Create it, and sell it to them. You ask, but how do you find that out, you can look in the book called SRDS, and find particular magazines, newsletters, mailing lists, TV, and radio stations. For example, you look for magazine on the type of hobby you like. Let's say you golf. There's a few magazines on golf or there's a mailing list of golfers, in you see, what these people have bought, how much money they spent, and when the last time they bought something. There's thousands of people to sell to. Example. The people I sell to, are the people that want to start a business. And people that already own business. This is a large group to sell to. You can sell to any group of people. Just make sure you like what you sell. The more specific, you are, the more money, you can get. Example. If you have a course on time, management. If you're lucky, you might get let's say $69. But if you make it, time management for the CEO of electrical power company, then you can charge $299 and up.

Track how much money you spend, and use a spreadsheet, and be consistent about it. You must know how much money you spend, and how much money comes in. You want to know that if you spend $10, it brought back $110. Not only do you want to know how much money. It brought back, but also from where. Where the money came from. Let's say, you've placed 50 ads in 50 different magazines and you spend about $100,000; made $400,000. If you don't keep track, how will you know that the 25 of the magazines your ads are in, don't work, and losing money. Keep track so you know, in the example you could've been making $800,000. But because you didn't know, you'll need to find systems to keep track. The computer is a vital tool.

Analyze the market, compare one market against another market. Keep track of what is happening. Because this way, you keep your self from making a costly decision. And read. Leaders are readers, but not all readers are leaders. Want you to read, magazines that you or customers or clients read. I like to read Fortune magazine, small-business opportunity magazine, business 2.0, entrepreneur magazine, and etc. etc. read what you like to read. This way, your mind is always analyzing and comparing, where the market is going, what action to take to make more money. What action to stop, so that you don't lose money. Yes, those are commonsense thinks, but if you don't know how you will do what you don't know. Like I said, commonsense is not as common. What if you see the marketing headed in a certain direction, and because you are an action taker. You can implement strategies to make you the most money, and to take the biggest market share than the competition, it's always good.

$5000-$25000, how much money is your customer worth. Let's say in one year, three years, five years, or a lifetime. It's important to know, how much your customer will spend with you, because then you will have a basic figure of how much money. You'll spend to get that customer. If your customer spends $10,000 in three years, then it wouldn't be a big thing to spend $1000 to acquire that customer. The money is not in the initial purchase, but it's in the purchases thereafter. It will take time to know how much each person is worth to you. Again, this goes back to, keep track of what people spend, and how much they spent and on what they spent on. You need a computer to track and put customers in different categories. This technique, I learned from Dan Kennedy. I recommend you buy all of Dan Kennedy's books. Courses and if you can consult with him for an hour, do ti. Keep track of what the customer is worth to you.

Multiply your earning power, by using up sales. Let's say, you had the person called an operator to request a free report. Will you would say, yes, will include your report. And for an extra $10, will send you a video that now normally sells for $49.95, but because you called, will only charge $10 for. This script can be used when leads call for the information. But here's another scenario, the customers calling and places a $500 order. You can have a script that says, we will process you order, but we have another product would like to give you a half-price. The normal price is $500, but for limited time only. It's only $250, and shipping is free. Now instead of only making $500, you have now made $750 with the initial purchase. How many people will buy? It always depends on your market, your offer, and the price. Let's say that 20% of the people buy. That means out of a hundred customers. You're able to make an extra $5,000. You didn't have. You can use this process on the internet too, and put it on automatic.

Big money is all in the back end of the process. What's back end? That's when you sell more products to the client. After they bought the initial product. When you deliver the product. Your clients now trust you, and it's much easier to get your customer to buy from you again. Let's say, you're selling a manual and six CDs for $297. Initial product. When you send the package, include a sells letter for another, more expensive package let's say, $997, if out of a hundred customers, 10% by the more expensive package. That's $9,970 extra into your bank account. And out of the 10% of people that bought the more expensive package. You sell them a $5,000 package, and let's say 10% buy, that's an extra $5,000. Make this a process in your business. Always be selling more products, more often, and more expensive. You make millions of dollars with this process. You start with a $20 book or an audio book, then $97 for three CDs. Then $497 for a manual with CDs and one video. $2500 for the life-changing seminar that you're going to sell them. The process is never ending.

Creating informational products takes time. The way to save time and money is to license other people's products. There's three types of licenses. Number one master reprint licenses, number two. Reprint licenses, and number three, resale license. The master reprint rights can make you a ton of money. You can easily spend $15,000 for the master reprint rights for a package that sells for $5,000. Master reprint rights, give you the right to sell to other, so they can sell it to others. Example, you buy a master reprint to a package called secrets of tycoon millionaires. Home study course. You invest $15,000 in the package. And you sell the reprint rights to your friend for $5, 000, that means that your friend now can sell the package for $997, and can't pass the reprint rights to anyone else. The type of licensing deals I'm talking about our royalty free, meaning you never have to pay royalty fees. Second type of license is reprint rights, this is where you buy a package and reproduce it, and you selling keep all the money. The last type of license is resale rights. This is when you sell the package in key between 25% to 50% or even 75% of the money collected. Beginning in on one of these types of deals is good for you. This way you can sell products, make money, and then later create your own products to sell. The secrets of these licensing deals is to make sure you get the marketing pieces that, together with your package, because without the sells letters. You can't sell products. It's very difficult to create a sells letter. You can create a sells letter or get someone else to write it for you.

Reward yourself, to keep you motivate. Buy the car of your dreams, so when you see it. You feel excited, and motivated to keep going. Take vacations, refresh yourself. Making money is fun, but you must reward yourself. So that you don't get burned out. When I make my first $10 million I'm going to buy the Rolls-Royce Phantom. This is my motivator, when you make your first $1 million. How are you going to reward yourself? What places are you going to go to? What House Will you buy? What type of jewelry will you get? Keep motivated it's important part of your growth, not only in business, but also in your personal life. Read books on motivation. Listen to books on CD to keep motivated. Buy home study courses. Watch uplifting images. Listen to up lifting music. Without motivation. You won't want to take action, so invest in your motivation.

Tell people not to waste your time, like I said Time is a valuable asset use it wisely. If you don't want to be rude. act like your phone is on vibrate pick it up and excuse yourself of the persons presents that's wasting your time. If you have an office closed door. You could have a secretary, let her screen calls, avoid meetings if you can take a limo so you can have free time to do business, or even recharger batteries. Rich people aren't stuck up, because they have a jet that takes them to places. They take limousines, because these things are time maker. Going to the airport can take five hours out of your time. For one hour plane flight. Taking a limo, can give you extra hours of time to do business. Keep this in mind. People that waste your valuable asset, must be stopped. Be looking out for activities you can let someone else do for you, and free up your time to do business that brings you in billions or millions of dollars.

CHAPTER 6. Testing

Profit is the name of the game. The fastest way to do it, is to test. You'll test your advertising. Not only will you save money, but you'll know where to invest the money. So the thing you should do is test. Example, how many people will call this ad? "Free Report - Make Money Fast" As opposed to "Quick And Easy Money". Now you won't know until you test to see how many people have called the ads. Another thing to test is the price. The headline should be the first thing to test, then the subhead. The layouts. The order form. Keep in mind to test one variable at a time. Save every headline that grabs your attention. Keep it in the Journal. You know, the magazine you buy the newspapers you read whatever grabs your attention. Later on, when you're ready to write your headline. You can adapt to create your own ad. See what's working in a different industry and tested in your industry.

Selling, or knowing how to make the money comes in, the highest function. You want to sell what people want to buy. Exchange products for money, and not your time for money. Residual income is what you want. The book created can bring you money over and over. The movie, you make will bring you money over and over again. A song you write will give you money over and over again. So the highest function of business is selling. Then Kennedy, the famous copywriter charges $75,000-$100,000 to write a sells letter, and he wants a percentage of what you make. The hardest thing he has to do is to have a serious face when he goes to collect his money. So learn every technique on selling in every strategy on selling keep track of what works better and better.

Top 20% of your clients will give you 80% of your revenue. The same as opposite, 80% of your headaches come from the bottom 20% of the customers that spend the least amount of money with you. So get rid of the bottom 20%, including the bottom 20% of your employees. The percent of your employee expenses, from the bottom 20% of the employee that bring you little or breakeven performance for your money. So get rid of them. This technique, I learned from Jack Welch of GE. He would fire these employees or reassigned them with this technique Jack was able to keep GE very profitable and competitive. So with this rule, pay close attention to the top 20% of your clients that bring you in the most money and fired 20% of your employees that don't bring value and fired the bottom 20% of customers that give you the most headaches and the least amount of money. The tricky part is figuring out, who are the top 20% and who are the bottom 20%.

Do evaluate your opportunities to make money.

If you invest $5,000 to see if your project will work. And you lose it. This money isn't a big deal. You didn't lose $500,000. The good thing is that you took action, evaluated and did not let your fear stop you. The name of the game is to make money with the least amount of risk, but in the real world. No risk equals no goodies. Many business people took a risk, a leap of faith. Read all of the biographies on billionaires and millionaires. To see what I mean, just keep in your mind, what you want to accomplish. Just stay on course in your mind, you will attract everything needed, and this technique can be used for your personal life, and your business life.

Watch how you spend your money. Keep track of your money. In other words, be frugal. If you're not careful. You can waste large amounts. Always know how much money you have. Always track where your money goes, be careful not to develop bad habits. Habits can make you poor. All ways get least three quotes on whatever you want to buy, whether it's a product or service, but keep in mind on quality, cheapest doesn't mean the best quality. If you spend five hundred dollars on a product, and it breaks four times. You just spent $2000 to have it replaced. The best quality would cost you only $1000. So you have to evaluate analyze, and be frugal with your money. Frugality keep to keep you rich.

Solutions to problems are what you want to bring

to people. Sell to people's interest. Keep in mind this phrase, if you help people get what they want, they will help you get what you want. This phrase will make you rich. Always create value for others. Always keep in the back of your mind solutions to people's problems. Business is not a step-by-step 1-2-3 process. It's in multiple levels. It's a big mess and process number eight might start before, number two business is like a human body. Every single sell, organ is working to keep you alive and growing. Everything in your body is working all at the same time. Not one by one step 1-2-3, but all at the same time. So keep in mind, look for solutions to people's problems and get rich.

Laws can help your business. Or they can hurt your business. It's very important when you're company grows into a large company. It's vital that you set money aside to give to the politicians, in other words, you must lobby so that politicians will pass laws to help your business. If you don't lobby. This can also hurt your business, because the politicians. You should have given money to, can pass laws or make decisions to hurt your business. Look at what happened to Microsoft's. They did lobby, but didn't give enough money, because a few years ago. Microsoft was slapped with the antitrust law suit. So keep in mind. When you're company starts to make billions of dollars. You must give it to politicians to let them know that you will help them, and you want to be helped, money gets money. I don't mean give all your billion away, but I do mean a certain percentage.

Get yourself focusing on positive results. This will give you the motivation. To keep going, an important part of your psychological process to be successful. Keep the big picture in mind, if you focus on failure, then that what you'll get. If you focus on success that's what you get, but here's something that will cleared up for you. More. I want you to change how you think about the Word failure. Failure doesn't exist. Only the Word results. If it's not the results you want, then change your action, to get the results you want. The Word failure is such a word that makes you feel bad, and its stock in your negativity. So if you switch the Word failure, and the Word success to the Word results and you won't be a successful person with positive results.

Time is one of the most valuable assets you have , so you must learn to multiply it. The only way to multiply time is to think about your efforts, and people to give you their efforts. The higher amount of money can be made if you think of how to multiply their effort. Lets look at how an MLM company grows. They use multiplication. They start out by teaching one-person. This person turns around and teaches another 10 people to sell the product and services. Teach 10 more people, so now you have 10 times 10 equals 100 and you have these people under the other people. Each teach 10 people. A hundred times 10 equals a thousand is a great system. Let's look at McDonalds. They sell a cookie-cutter system. Therefore multiplying their efforts. Burger King does the same. Think of ways to multiply your time and efforts.

Companies, friends and people you know, can also help you grow your business. You need to make friends with people that run companies that have what you need to grow your business. For example, if I was a company that made blockbuster superhot movies. I would have to be friends with a lot of CEOs of other companies to make my movie projects successful. Because I need to be able to distribute my movies to the theaters. The person that runs the theaters will give me better service, if he or she was my friend. I mean, the CEOs of retail outlets to sell my products. If these people are my friends. It will be easy to do business with them. So always network, and make friends with people that have influential jobs. You'll see your life easier and easier. Of course, you have to make friends with people that will help you in your industry or your future.

Research, sell, and deliver your products on the Internet. A whole lot of people are becoming not only millionaires, but billionaires on the Internet. If you wanted to see what people search for than go to www.adwords.google.com and use their search tool. To do some research. Remember first, refined a market, then we create the product. That they want to buy. If you've created an e-book, video, or audio. Not only will you get rich, but you can deliver it electronically. The Internet is an amazing tool. If you've never been on the Internet, then it's time to learn or you'll get left behind. You're not a left behind person, are you? Of course not. Once a friend of mine was going to hire a CEO to run his company. All my friend had to do is go to www.google.com and search the persons named and find out everything about the person, to see if he was the person he was looking for. You don't have to know anything about HTML, java, Scripts, or anything else about the Internet to use it. All of these technical stuff you can hire people to do those things for you.

Computers and the Internet have made the world , a smaller place, that means you can now do business all over the world, because it's cheaper to do it, won't cost hundreds of thousands to sell globally. The only thing you have to think about is language barrier, but you can hire translators to translate your information. Look at the book series chicken soup for the soul. It's been translated into a lot of languages, bringing more money to the table. Guests, you can now think and sell to the whole world. It's really amazing. You and I have the best opportunities in any generation, because of the technology. But even though there is all this technology still remember, you're dealing with people, and people have buying triggers. Don't be fooled with the technology. Business, big or small. It's all about selling what people want to buy. The Internet has made it very easy to start your empire, and build it.

The Bajamas comes to my mind of where on earth, has the lowest corporate tax. Transfer your corporation to an offshore company, to protect your wealth from the government. I have to give my disclaimer, I'm not an attorney, if you need one please hire one. Large corporations have shielded billions of dollars from the government, and yes, it's legal until the government passes new tougher tax laws. I'm not saying don't pay taxes, I'm saying is pay the least amount as possible. Like I said before, learn how to protect your money from individuals, the governments, and anyone else that's trying to take it from you. Many times, you'll be attacked, but if you are, prepared, it won't hurt. Always be on the lookout for companies, and people, and ideas that can help you keep your money.

Take action, and be firm with people that want to take advantage of you. Learn to say no! And learn to to have a thick skin, to fire people, and let friends go. People, if you give them an arm, if you let them, they'll take the other arm too. This tactic can be learned. Just think like this, that person doesn't care about me, and my situation. So I have to protect myself against the enemy.

Yes, it's pretty crude, but you must be firm with people. Don't worry about how it makes them feel. Some people learn the hard way, and when you fire someone, don't feel guilty, because there's 250,000 job categories that people can do. Guild is not a necessity, it's a choice. In your life. It's not needed. Remember, you're a business person. That wants to make a ton of money. And you need the correct people, and correct skills.

Lots of money can be made from selling your company. When you sell your company, you can find other, better and bigger opportunities. Keep your eyes open for better business opportunities. You can do and have so much more in business. If you start from your little business with $1000 and 36 months you have a billion-dollar business. It depends how ambitious, you are. You can sell your one billion-dollar revenue business for five to 10 times its value. Do the math. If your business is making one billion a year. You can sell it for $5,000,000,000-$10,000,000,000. And you can put all that money into your account. You can take half the money and invest in stocks, real estate, commercial real estate, bonds. Remember you are the best money manager. Never trust someone else with your money. Like I said before, you are your own best money manager. You'll never steal from yourself. If you don't want to sell your company. Then you'll only work until you die.

CHAPTER 7. Your Mind

You want to have an edge over others, and the only tool you have is your brain. Keep it sharp. Always be learning new ideas, and be open minded to hear both sides of the story. Example, if you read the Bible, then read the Koran. This might be against your norm, but like I said, keep an open mind. Evaluate the information, not judging it at the first. Once you've expanded you're mind. It will never shrink back down to its original size. When reading a book look for ideas that will help you. When you listing to others, ask yourself will this information help me? How will it help me? How can it help me? You'll be surprised at what new ideas, you get. Because if you find one simple idea and adapted to your business. It could mean millions or billions of dollars to you.

Allowing success into your life is a real problem. It comes down to your spirituality. Asking in meditation, what do you want, and thanking the infinite creation. The infinite creation for me is called God. So give thanks to what you call a higher self. Remember, we all made up of just energy, energy that vibrates in a certain speed. Water vibrates lower, but if it's heated it vibrates faster, and turns into steam. So for you to have abundance. You must first have it in your mind. So you can attract all the people and resources to you.   I learned this from Bob Proctor, I recommend Bob's book called: The power to have it all.

Reward yourself. At the beginning of the year. Plan out your whole year, but plan your vacation first. Then what you have to do to make money. It's a lot of fun to plan your vacation first, and you'll be looking forward to your vacation. By taking time off, you rejuvenate your energies, and give your brain time to digest new ideas that come to you. It's funny how people plan, what they do first is make money and then vacation. Plan your fun first. Think of where you want to go, how long you'll stay. Will you fly, or drive. Will you take a cruise. If you're going to fly. Then prearrange your transportation from, and to the airport, will you rent a limousine, or a cab, or take the shuttle bus. I recommend, take a limousine.

Knowing that God exists is important. By now you have build your own opinion about the creator. But remember, when you were little. You knew in your heart that God existed. Did you know that if one cone is off in your eye, you couldn't see in color. Look all around you. There's a higher power, keeping us on this planet. Just think about it, how fast is the earth spinning on its axis, did you know that scientists don't know what keeps an atom together. It's power of God. You don't have to take my word for it, but I want you to be successful, so you must get all the ideas. I know this will help you get abundance, or whatever else you want. Read the Bible. Pray for what you want. Remember, God can do miracles in your life. Always just give thanks to your higher power. If at all, just be spiritual.

Wherever you are, you can talk to the higher self. You can talk to your higher self. Whenever, you must allow any type of response to come back to you. It might be a word, a sentence, a dream or situation that happens to you, or it can be another person telling you something. The higher self can communicate with you in many different forms, but know this. Your higher self is always listening. Talking to God should be a natural conversation as if you were talking to another person. Like I said God is everywhere, all the time. The reason God lets so many bad things happen, there's two reasons. One, God gives you free choice to do whatever you wanted and the second reason is, you've requested something, and the only way to learn what you've requested is for something bad to happen to answer your request. I learned it the hard way, nowadays. I'm very careful what I asked for.

Books are great to read. You should read as many books as possible. A book, you should read once is the Bible. So you can come up with your own conclusions about the spiritual side of you. Another place to learn about the Bible is in a school. All depends how much you want to learn. Yes, this is a business book, and your spirituality has a lot to do with your wealth. If you think poor, them you'll be poor, but if you think Rich. You will be rich. The Bible should be read with an open mind, no prejudice. The Bible was written by man, but inspired by God. You know, god talks to you every day, but we're not listening. There's too many distractions, such as, the TV, work, your family, the radio, etc. etc. anything that distractions from guide is a sin, what I want you to know about your spiritual self, because the Bible is a spiritual guide. Don't let what I said stop you from becoming wealthy, God wants you to be wealthy.

Positive thought is what you want to have while meditating. You should meditate in a quiet place every day. For about 20 minutes. You can think of nothing. Just be blank, or you can think of oneness. What I do is meditate for the first 20 minutes in the morning, then I go about my business. If you don't know how to meditate you can pick up a book. At the library, or at the bookstore. You can learn to meditate on your own. It's not a mysterious thing to do. When you meditate, you won't feel weird or crazy, or anything else like that. The reason, meditate it is to keep yourself at the higher vibration. If you want to make $8 billion a year. You meditate every day for 20 minutes on making $8 billion a year, and you'll see all the resources coming to you, because you are vibrating in the thought of making $8 billion a year.

Twenty-one days is what it takes to embrace a new habit. A way to get new habits is to use hypnosis. It's very easy to do. You must relax your entire body. Then think in the presence. Example, if I want to lose 20 pounds of fat. I wouldn't say, I don't want to be fat. Instead I would say. I am happy and grateful now that I have released 20 pounds. And if you write the sentence down   100 times a day by hand. Repetition affects a subconscious mind. If you're going to use hypnosis, I recommend you work one thought at a time. Or one subject that time. There's many hypnotic programs in the market. There is programs on prosperity, weight loss, confidence, better speaking, and etc. I'll break it down for you. Number one, feel your whole body relaxing, that's what the induction script is for to relax you. Number two, tilt your eyes up at 45° angle. Number three fantasize about what you want, see it happening in the present tense. Number four, add feelings to what you're fantasizing about. Number five, repeat twice a day, once in the morning, and once before you go to sleep.

Tired, feeling low on energy, then it's time to take a nap. You can do a 20 minute nap, midmorning or whenever you need it. All the great geniuses had naps throughout the day. Use this new habit to help you. Naps will give you an extra boost of energy. If you don't do that now, then try at lunchtime. Instead of eating, take a nap or take a nap on your 15 minute break. If you're the boss. You can decide when to take a nap. In Japan, the workers are instructed to take a one-hour nap. They've proved that it makes people produce more, feel energized, and more, and less stress. Naps vital part of becoming a tycoon in any field. Make sure no one bothers you when you're napping. There's a scientist that did a study. The scientist was able to stay up and functioned perfectly, by taking naps every four hours and 20 minutes times. If you do the math. He slept about four hours per day, but in 20 minute increments. You can try the same. If you want. My favorite word is test.

Take a massage once a week or once every two weeks. This help you released tons of toxins in your muscles and helps you feel good. Another thing is to get a massage after your work out. Your whole body will feel incredible. If you don't get massage than test it out. Don't always concentrate on how much it will cost. The thing to be aware of is the person that's going to massage to. Are they positive? You don't want a person that's negative massaging your body, because I feel that their bad energy will transfer into your body. I don't want that, and also the person has to be clean. How's their hygiene, they look healthy, they smell clean? Whatever else you can think of. Do you want a man to massage or do you want a woman to massage you. So that you don't feel uncomfortable. Make sure you have the right person massaging you.

Try to have pleasing odors around you. Just remember how a certain smell makes you feel. Does it give you energy? Does it make you feel sad? Does it make you happy? Does it make you feel relaxed. Keep a log of how you feel and only have the odors that give you energy, and make you feel powerful. Not only will you benefit from it, but others will too. Aromatherapy sounds like you might be sick, but you don't have to be thinking like that. Remember anything that gives you a slight edge is what we are looking for. If you feel out of energy, you must look at many different things. Your diets, your thoughts, are you eating, getting enough rest, are you drinking enough water. What people are sucking up to much energy. Are there any unpleasant smells? Do you feel clean? Whatever it is you must take care of it, cut it to make things happen. You need a lot of energy.

Positive or negative colors can also affect your state of mind. Colors can make you feel powerful or weak. Example, when you go to the hospital do you knows the colors around, greens, blues, purples, like colors. Why? Because there's been a study that these colors make people relax and heal faster. The color you should have in the room you sleep in his white, or a little bit off white. Because this color will help you relax the most. Don't make your room black, red, or yellow. These colors affect your mood and your thoughts. Also the color of your car is important, don't get the fun colors like yellow, light green, light blue, any fluorescent color, because people won't take you seriously. Another thing the best colors to wear is black suits . Second black suit with red pinstripes, next is navy blue suit with light blue shirt and a red tie. You'll notice how people treat you. These colors command respect.

Yoga is a good form of exercise to do, because it helps stretch and massage the whole body. Now when I say your whole body. I mean your organs, your nerves etc. You must choose, what style you'll do. You can do the traditional, or you can do power yoga, and everything else. I do the traditional. When you start, you'll notice a difference of how you act and feel. You'll be more energized. The special glands around your body are affected, the most. These glands control How much certain chemicals are released into your body. There's plenty of books on yoga, and there's plenty of classes, you can take, or you can buy a video on yoga. Do it once in the morning after your physical work out. These activities will help you to live longer and be healthier and you'll be sick less. What's the difference between fit and healthy? Fit is your physical strength, and healthy is your well-being.

Don't have to much sex, because that's energy. This energy should be transmute into getting things done. If you are going to have sex, make sure the other person is as smart as or smarter than you. I know what I'm about to say may sound strange, but listen, when you have sex with someone, it's like your mind connects, and take from the other persons mind, and you'll become smarter. It's like that movie called "The Highlander " where you cut your opponents head off and you get their life force and knowledge, having sex is much more fun than killing someone. Sex is also a powerful motivator. I know of some guys that will have a family, and will buy the fanciest car, the most expensive car. Just to attract the woman he wants. Like I said, sex is a powerful motivator. Think what you would do to have sex, how much successful must you to get a certain type of partner. Use this to motivate you.

CHAPTER 8. Your Manifestation

Better think big, to get what you want, because if you get 10% of $1 billion. You'll still be OK. You're going to do things anyways, why not think big, the bigger you think, the more motivating you get. Not only that, but your subconscious mind will be working to get what you want. Thinking big will allow you as a person to accomplish much more than thinking small. Have big dreams, because thoughts are things. You never know how wonderful your life can get, unless you think really big. Not only can you think big about money, but you can think big about your house, the cars, the planes, and everything else that you want. Go ahead and fantasize in a big way.

Life is a series of questions, the better answers you get the better life you'll have. Before you answer the question. Concentrate on your good thoughts, and come up with a question. The only question I don't ask when bad things happen to me is why did this bad thing happened to me? This question can be self-defeating, instead ask. What can I do to fix it? Or if someone does something bad, try to find out what's good about. Ask this question, what is good about this? Or, what could be good about this situation? If you asked the wrong question. Then you'll get the wrong answer, if you asked the smart question. Then you'll get a smart answer. You never know what question will change your life.

Close your eyes to see what you want. This process is called visualization. Before you can have it in your life, you must have it in your mind. Let's do an exercise. (After you read do it), close your eyes and see something very simple. How about a ball, a tennis ball, you see it. It's green, with two lines through it. How about the chair? See it? See it in detail. Start with small objects, and keep it in your mind as long as possible. Then you can start to visualize your goals. See how it's going to be, but in your imagination. It has to be in the present tents. Your mind won't know the difference. OK. Let me give you another example. Think of the best sex, you ever had. How is the other person kissing? Do you feel the sensations? The hear, the sounds? What about the skin. How are you feeling? Imagine this for a while. Do you see what I mean? You're experiencing the feelings as if you were there. Visualize everything you want.

Manifestation is the process that occurs when you write down what you want. Different goals have different digestion times. To happen in your life. I want you to write down 101 things you want, you want to be, you want to do, and what you want to have. Don't worry how you'll accomplish any of these 101 goals. Just write them down. The first 65 to 75 things will be easy to come up with, but to reach 101 things, it's going to be tough. Don't worry. You can take up to three days to think about 101 things on paper, but the most important thing is, to write it down. Writing it down is the first process of manifestation. What you want? It's an easy and fun exercise to do. Like I said, don't worry how you'll accomplish any of it. Let your subconscious mind worry about this. You'll be surprised what and how things will start to happen in your life. Just do the exercise 101 things.

Storyboard is a valuable tool to use to make movies. It lets everyone know what needs to be done next, its a series of pictures put together to tell the story. There's the beginning, there's the middle, and there's the end, it's easy to do, just past pictures of what you want to happen in your life. The storyboard is kind of a reminder for your subconscious and conscious mind. It said that the wealthiest man in the United States of America, uses storyboard to accomplish his goals. He runs a very successful software company. It's been said that he has over 1600 storyboard. Of his goals. That's a lot, but as you accomplish each one the next goal is being worked on in your mind. It's kind of what I call the popcorn effect. Have you ever watch how popcorn pops? You put the un-popped corn into a big pan, and you apply heat. When enough pressure and heat is made it pops open, and the next one pops open, in the meantime, heat is being applied until it all pops. Your attention is like the heat that pops the goals out.

Manifest your ideas and goals takes a certain type of person, you should write down what you're perfect day looks like. From the moment you wake up, to the moment you go to sleep. When you have your perfect day written out, read it once in the morning, and once at night. You're getting a lot of ideas to help you manifest your goals. The psychology on using is the more techniques to use the faster your goals will manifest. Just like the more gas you give to your car, the faster it goes. All of the techniques given to you all are given to influence your subconscious mind. Your subconscious mind has the key to unlocking all that you want. Nightingale Cole and said that you become what you think about the most, because it affects the subconscious mind

Realize we all make mistakes and to fix your mistakes. You must first know what they are before, you can fix it. Common sense. So for you to realize the hidden mistakes of your life. Here's a question. You should answer. What is holding you back? Write down everything you can think of. After this exercise, you're going to be surprised that what's holding you back. Then you'll be able to fix it. The best way is to just realize what's holding you back. Example. What's holding back from becoming a billionaire? Here the answers that came to me, I would lose my friends, I would have to move, and my family may not like me. This is what you have to say to yourself. If I lose a friend than that person wasn't really my friend. I'll make new friends. If I have to move, but I don't have to stay. If my family doesn't like me, it's OK, it can influence everyone. It's their choice. Your going to have to answer your own questions to fix your own problems. Ask the right questions.

Attracting what you want simply comes down to how you're vibrating. A piece of ice vibrates at a certain speed to be a solid piece of matter, if you apply energy to it. It turns into water and that vibrates at a certain speed. If you keep applying energy. It turns into steam, and if you continue applying energy, it will turn to either. So energy travels from solid to either. The same way your thoughts travel from your spiritual self, to your intellectual self, into your physical self. That's why it's important to think and focus on the things you do want, so that you're vibrating at a certain cycle and attracting all the resources to manifest your goals. Example. If few years ago. I wrote the words. I'm a billionaire, in the morning that was the first thing I would read and before going to sleep. After a year later , I met, and worked with three multibillionaire that have opened my eyes. I'm vibrating like a billionaire, because that's what I focus on, and think about the most. The law of attraction, can help you or it can hurt you. If you focus on not being broke, the mere fact that you are focusing on the words broke, will manifest into your life. So think of rich and abundance only.

Have it in your mind before you can have it in you life. Whatever you think about the most, tend to happen. If you think about not having enough money and you think I don't want to have my money run. That's what you'll get. No money. If you've thought I hope I don't get fired that's what you'll get. If you keep thinking on the negative things, than that's what will keep happening to you. Until you start thinking of what you do want, in a positive tents. Instead of thinking, I don't want to be broke. Think I make $100 million a month easily. What you think about the most will happen, like a self-fulfilling prophecy? What happens is, that you start to turn into a magnet. Whatever thoughts you think about the most, become energized, and it attracts the situations. You were thinking about the most. That's why it's vital that you pay attention to your thoughts.

Persistence is a habit, you'll definitely need. If you don't have it. What you have to do, is get motivated. Here's an exercise. Write down why you want a successful business? Write down how you will feel? Write as vividly as possible. Here's a quote that will help you. "Positive mental habits, apply through persistent correct action, will get you what you want." Your whole success, your whole life, begins, and ends, with your thoughts. Not someone else's thoughts.

So always be thinking, and analyzing what you think about the most. Your mind is your genie in the lamp. Your mind can and does grant wishes. So have a plan to take persistent correct action. And yes, you need to be persistence, and have discipline.

Prison is not a nice place to go. When you cause another person harm in any way shape or form, you can go to prison. It's important for you to be a good person to everyone that deserves it. Some people dislike you, but don't worry about them, because more people will like you, then dislike you. Keep your business and personal life, honest. Honesty is the good for your soul, and it will keep you out of prison. Don't judge a person that's gone to prison. Did you know that if you hire an ex-felon your company can get a tax break from the IRS. The government can help pay half of his or her salary. Contact your local agencies. To find out how you can benefit from hiring an ex-felon. Now, not every ex-felon that will be a good choice, some of the people that have gone to prison will be very angry at what happened to them. Instead of forgiving their situation, they keep it inside, and kill any opportunity that comes their way. Remember only hire ex-felons that what to change their life for the good.

Thinking that life is not fare, will be just that. Because you're attracting it. If you have a negative miserable attitude, than that's the life your going to have. The miserable negative dark life. Isn't it better to think positive to think the world is giving. Every good thing in life. The world is a great place to be. If you know people that are negative, keep yourself at a distance from these negative people. Because you'll get infected with their diseases, per se. Negative people suck up a lot of energy from themselves and others. The only way to be immune is to not be with these types of people. If you know these people have limited amount of contact with them. If you have a friend like this, you definitely understand what I'm talking about. No matter what, get rid of them. Make new friends, with positive, or at least neutral people.

Firm positive mental habits, are your friends. Accept that there's people out there that will want you to have bad habits. Stay away from these people that want to influence you to do negative things, like drinking, or making you late for appointments, or anything else that will hurt you. Some people may not do it on purpose, but they're doing it subconsciously. That's why their life doesn't go so good. It's very important to have friends that are positive and successful, if not more successful than you. So that you can pick up good habits from them. Let me tell you a little story, the other day I came out of a restaurant and a homeless guy asked me for some change, and I gave him all the loose change in my pocket. I stood there talking to him and tried to get him to think positive, as I start to leave this old homeless woman. She said to me, "The homeless, take care of the homeless." That statement made me think millionaires take care of millionaires. Billionaires take care of Billionaires. Basically success people help, successful people.

Chemicals affect what and how you think. Sugar also has this affect, and medicine has the same affect. It's important to be sober, from medicine and chemicals, for you to think the best thoughts for business, and personal situations. Talk to a person on medicine or drugs, and you'll see they're not themselves. Talk to a person on some kind of drug and talk to a person that's eating too much sugar. Remember what you want to be is a successful business person, not a homeless unsuccessful miserable person. You have to decide not to take drugs, chemicals, too much sugar, or too much medicine into your body. The human body was created perfect. Your body has everything it needs to heal itself. As long as you take the proper foods and proper mental thoughts.

Drinking alcohol is another bad habit. If you drink, stop. If you smoke, stop. If you do drugs, stop. All of the substance will hurt you in the long run. You might think you need them, but you don't. Live your life in a productive way, so that when you're on your last breath. You can think, I've lived a productive healthy life, to my best ability possible. I can go in peace.

Hopefully, you'll be very old. I have a goal to live to be 200 years old. So I don't smoke. I don't drink, and don't do any drugs. In the near future medical advances will help a person live to be 200 years old or more, but if your brain has been bombarded with drugs, alcohol, and smoke. What's the use of living to be 200 years old? If your mind is lost. By not using any of these things you'll have an edge over people that do drugs, drink and smoke.

CHAPTER 9 Protecting it

Tell people that are difficult, that you just don't have the time for them. Just walk away. Act busy, if you have to, just walk away from difficult people. If they work for you, fire them. If they are clients fire them. There's too many good people out there, to replace these difficult people. Whether it's an employee, or customer, replace them with good people. Better customers. Think of the 20 80 principal. Concentrate on the top 20% of your employees, concentrate on the top 20% of your customers. Get rid of the bottom 20% of your customers, and get rid of the bottom 20% of your employees, because these people will drain your efforts. You don't want to get infected with their bad habints. Life will be much easier once you get rid of these difficult people. It's always in your best interest to be surrounded with good productive people.

Money is the name of the game. So it's vital to get rid of non-productive people. Because they are like a disease, and they will infect productive healthy people, with their bad habits. unproductive people are a waste of your money. Needless to say. In the beginning, you'll have to go through and shuffle, shifting of people to find good people. What I recommend his to fire fast, higher slow. Slow because you want to get to know the people, and get to see how they act. You are responsible for the people in your company. Don't feel guilty. When you have to fire people, because there's 250,000 job categories that people can do. You're just helping them find what they are good at. Only hire productive people around you, and don't waste your time, money, and energy on unproductive people.

Big headaches can be avoided. When you spot fake people. Fake people can make your life miserable. Fake people cannot be around you, and your money. Fake people cannot be trusted with anything of confidence, and privacy. Fake people are not your friends. They're just looking out for themselves. Fake people are easy to spot, you can notice them by what they say, and how they act. Sometimes, how they dress. Sometimes even by the colognes or perfume, they wear. It's easy to spot a fake guy. It's difficult to spot a fake female. I don't mean fake as in fake breasts. I mean a person that will say and do anything to gain your trust and then back stab you, the second they think they'll gain an edge. You've seen it in the movies, and you've seen it in real life. Pay attention.

Appointments must be made for every person that you know, will waste your time, and when you have them at the appointments, put them under a timer of 15 minutes. People that have a timer will tell you everything you need to know in

15 minutes, instead of 60 minutes. Also tell people that you know that waste your time, to be courteous of your time. An excellent book, I recommend is called. No B.S. time management, by Dan Kennedy, get this book, and use the ideas in that book. Time is the most valuable asset you have, so learn how to stop people from wasting your valuable (asset) time. Another way to interrupt people is take a call an excuse yourself from their presence. Keep your office door close, this way, it will discourage people that want to waste your valuable time. Another technique is to have an office away from your office, because if they can't find you, then they can't waste your time.

Cut off the people that want to waste to much of your energy. Tell these energy sucking people that you are too busy for them, unless they are going to bring you tremendous amounts of value. Your body and brain are like batteries, and you must be careful how you spend your energy. Some people don't know that they suck people's energies. Next thing you know, your worn out. Protect what energy you have, and cut off the people that want to waste it. The word waste, is such a nasty word. Don't let your energy, time, and talent go to waste. You want to be remembered as a person that did good deeds and produce tremendous amounts of value. Keep a look out for people you know, or people you feel would waste your energy. It's a form of disrespect. People, if you let them will waste your time, money, talents, and your life. Don't let it happen. Be firm with these people to preserve your valuable energy.

Interrupt people that complain too much. It's your choice, and your right, not to listen to people that complain. Again, these people are people that want to infect your mind with negativity. You know what I tell these people. I tell them, look I have my own problems to deal with, and I don't want to hear your problems. You have a choice of what happens to you. Tell these people right away, even if they are your friends, or family member. Don't get exposed to these people's negative energy. Just stay away from these types of people. You'll notice the people that complain the most, have a miserable life. You can see. They don't make enough money. Their attitude is always nasty. Their life doesn't go the way they want. But little they know, they brought, and attract their own existence. Although negative, they are still responsible. You are not responsible for their life.

Anger is another type of energy, you don't want. Especially from another person. The time to walk away from a person that is angry, rude and has no consideration should be right before your temper reaches a point of violence. When that happens just walk away from the person that is angry, disrespectful, and rude to you. You should know what you're tolerance level is, and it doesn't matter who you walk away from. It can be your friend, family, or other. Especially people you don't know. Again, this comes down to your keeping your energy to be able to put it to productive use. People can be so messed up, your job is to keep all people that are going to hurt you in your pocket or people that want to waste your money, time, and energy. Also be looking out for people that can add value to your life.

Stubborn, arrogant people are another group of people to be ignored. These people don't deserve your attention, time, or energy. It doesn't matter who they are or what they've done. People should treat all people with respect, unless the other person does something to hurt you. You should treat all people with respect, until they do something wrong to you. If you know this person from other people, and you've heard how they treat others, just stay away. Deal with arrogant people with little time as possible. People that tell me. You know, who I am? I tell them. It's not important to me at this time to know who you are. You'll get on unfavorable response, but just walk away, and if they come to your office call security. Your life is very valuable, and don't let anyone waste your time. Don't waste your time with arrogant people.

Have you ever heard of guilty by association. Don't hang out with people bad reputations, because you'll catch the judgment, and bad habits. The only away, people don't judge you as bad, if you are with a celebrity type, and everyone knows that person's style. But for the most part, you'll be judged by your association. If you want to be respected, hanging out with people that command respect. Go to events, and charities were famous powerful people hand out, and be seen with them, take pictures with them, collaborate on projects, you can even hire these powerful people. This will help your image. If people, don't respect you, it's pretty hard to make them respect you, without using some type of violence. Remember, your going to be guilty by association. Be around other successful people.

Second time a person blows you off, just forget about them, and do with fast. Don't go out of your way with people that blow you off. It doesn't matter who they are, family, or person that want to do business with you. People that blow you off, are disrespecting you, don't waste your energy trying to get them to pay attention to you, because it won't do any use. You'll just get aggravated. Keep your mind at ease, always be protecting your thoughts. Don't let them get contaminated. Because of other people. Remember everything that happens to you, and whatever you think about, affects your subconscious mind. It's vital to protect what type of information gets to your subconscious mind. Example. If you ever had a dream about the situation, you were thinking about. See that the transfer into your subconscious mind. Protect it. Because it becomes your reality.

Talk to people, tell them what you want. Remember people are not psychic , you should tell people what you want during, before, and after your conversation with that person, or group of people. Remember, you want to be a success. Communicating with people that work under you, with you, or above you, should know what's on your mind, and the only way to do that is to talk to them, send notes, or memos. You can send e-mail, faxes, and even have your entire company on twitter.   Always be communicating so that everyone is on the same page, going the same direction.   Words are pretty powerful tool, use it wisely. If you say something really, really dumb, people can and do lose respect for you. If they lose respect, then you lose control. So it's vital to expand your vocabulary, not only to help you communicate, but help you think faster, and better.

Control your temper. Never yell at a person, because then you lose respect instantly, in effect, that person won't work as hard for you. It's best to have self-control and understanding of others.   But the moment you start to yell. You've lost. Don't put yourself in that position, if you think you're going to blow your top at someone. Tell excuse yourself out, or if they're in your office. Tell them you need a moment to yourself. There's many things to think about, but be careful what you do, so that others don't lose respect for you, trust, or confidence in your abilities to make things happen. Never let your leadership abilities be injured, because of what you did. Also watch what you don't do. As time goes on, you'll develop the six-sense about things. Go with your gut feeling, sometimes and watch what happens, you could be surprised.

Routinely be looking for better and better professionals, and workers to help you in your organization. Always be evaluating performance. Whether it's your attorney, accountant, manager, everyone. You never know what person will help you grow into the successful person you want to become. People are the most important part of a company. People are also important to what they buy from your company. No matter how big, or small, your business is. It's all about people. Getting people to work for you, or getting people to buy from you. It's all about people. So be on the look out for better people to work for you, better people, to buy what you were company has for sale. Also be looking out for people that have good ideas about products, or about doing a particular procedure that will save you money. Always be thinking about it, so that you will attract it into your life.

Worry about your problems, just a little bit, don't ponder about your problems, because then you become a magnet of negative energy, and more bad things will happen to you. It's like a never ending circle. So be careful what you think about, because what you think about, negative or positive, tends to happen. If you think the good thoughts most of the time, then most of the time you'll be perfect, everything will go great. If things don't go the way you want, learn from them. Analyze a bit, and move on to better more positive thoughts. It's very important to be thinking about what you do want, not on things you don't want. Because whatever you focus on happen. It's like a projector, the light in the projector is your energy. The film is your thoughts. Whatever type of film that passes through your projector will project on the canvas of your life. So it's important to have good positive thoughts.

Pain from a broken heart, has to be dealt with very quickly. Because it can affect your professional life. Don't listen to sad music, get busy. Keep your mind occupied, and just accept what has happened. Keep in mind as long as you're alive, you can decide to take different actions. It's when you were sick, or dead. Then you can do nothing about your situation. If the other person doesn't want to be with you, don't get hostile, don't use violence to change the person's mind. Just accept and say, the most powerful word, which is NEXT! So that the next wonderful person can come into your life. There's millions of people. You can attract to your life. If you're attracting a certain type of person you don't like, then just look inside of yourself. Like I said, whatever you think about, will come into your life. If you are attracting people you don't like just analyze what you think about. The most. And instead think about the exact person you want, and not the person you don't want.

CHAPTER 10 Power of the Internet

Global business is now easier than ever. Anyone that wants to sell outside the United States can do so through the help of the Internet. The Internet is not only a great tool to help you do research, but also to do business. Even if you don't have a large budget. Through the Internet now, the little guy can play with the big boy's. Learn how to use the Internet, if you've never been on the Internet, it's time to start. You have a lot of fun, not only can you do business, but you can find anything about the hobbies you like to know more about. The Internet has revolutionized how we can communicate with others at an affordable reach that everyone can use. The Internet can make you a millionaire overnight, working 24 hours to help sell your company's products and services. The same direct response marketing principles can be used online, just as effectively as off-line. Get acquainted with the Internet world, and take advantage of it.

Time management connectivity management is important to your success. A great tool to have and learn to use is the computer. The computer has revolutionized our lives without computers are lives won't be as good as it is now. Computers can save you time, computers can do difficult tasks at very high speeds. If you don't own a computer. It's time to get one. Don't be afraid of playing with the computer, if you brake it, you can fix it, or buy a new one. Computers are very affordable nowadays. You can buy system for about $300. Or you can buy a cheaper one, if it's used computers. Don't be left behind, because you don't believe in computers. Pretty soon, if you don't know how to use a computer in your life will be a hard one to live try to get claimed with the computer and software. Computers are necessary to learn and to conquer. Take advantage of it.

Cost, speed, and reliability are the things to think about when deciding to get Internet access.
Access is now affordable for everyone, star out with what you can afford. As time goes on and you start to make money in your company make sure you get faster and faster internet speeds. If you live in a town that offer fiber optic internet access, get it, if it fits your budget. Fiber optics has made the access of being online extremely fast and affordable. No matter what you need to be connect to the world wide web. Internet access is vital to your business existence.

Uptime is a very important considerations to keep in mind when you want to build an Internet site. Some hosting companies will guarantee 99.8% uptime and lots of services for $10 to $400 a month, don't be too concerned about the price of having a place to host you site, Because if your able to set a web site that makes about $5,000-$50,000 a month. If your site is down for one-day. You're losing a lot of money. So get the best that you can afford as you make money and get better and better service. The best that I can think right now is to go to http://www.backseatbillions.com/recommends to see which companies I recommend, because I'm always researching the best companies. If you want you can do your own hosting, I don't recommend it, because you're going to spend a lot of time thinking and wondering about the technical stuff, and fighting off hackers to your site, instead of making big money, let the hosting job be done by someone else.

Four-Hundred million dollars, that's what Disney spent on their web site. But because you are much smarter. You want to spend not even a fraction of that if you have time on your hands. You can learn to make your own web site. If you want to learn go to http://www.backseatbillions.com/recommends you can watch the videos. A good HTML program to help you design web site is Dreamweaver. It will take a just a few hours of practice and anyone can create a web site. If you don't want to spend the money to get Dreamweaver. You can get your free editing software, called Komposer. It's very easy to use. That was the first web site editing software, I used to make my first web site. You don't have be a technical genius to use it. Another thing to keep in mind when making web site is to use direct response marketing strategies.

Headline is the most important thing a person sees on your website. Next thing to think about is your offer and than make it easy to order? Let's talk about the headline, get a course on headlines just visit http://www.backseatbillions.com/recommends The headline has to make a person want to read the next line, and that line has to make the person want to read the next line, and so on, and so on until the sell is made. Start collecting headlines that grab your attention. You can get headlines out of magazines, newspapers, radio commercials, TV commercials and other websites. You have a strong headline presented to the right people, then you're going to make millions of dollars on your website. You should ask yourself a question before you rate your website, what do I want the person visiting to do once they get to the website being get their e-mail and contact information or get them to buy something make it easy for the person visiting to know what to do.

Six seconds is how long it should take for your website to load. If it takes longer than that. People lose patience and will go onto another website. The way to make you site load faster to the browser is not to use too many graphics because graphics take up a lot of memory. And besides graphics can distract a person from the sales message. Another way to make your site load faster is to break it out into smaller windows. If you visit www.marketingtips.com you'll see what I mean. When you look at the source page, what they did to make it go fast on minutes alone can kill your business. If it takes to long people will want just take a look at how you react when the website takes too long to load. Fast load speed is your friend when it comes to websites.

Paper click search engines are good way to bring traffic to your website. Another good way to bring traffic to your website is to advertise in e-zines the other great method. If done right can bring lots of traffic is banner ads don't know what pay per click search engines is just visit www.google.com and type keyword tool, and the type in a keyword bunch of website choices will appear as the number one website the first position because they were willing to spend the most amount of money to get a person to click on their website. Once people get to your website, offer to give them a free gift, it can be a video, it can be an mp3, or it can be an e-zine is it just an electronic newsletter delivered to the e-mail. A banner ad takes up a small room at the top of a webpage and flashes different ads you can pay $10 per thousand flashes. Or you can pay less, and all they depends on the company you use.

Test everything on the website to get the best

amount of conversions. A conversion is the amount of people that buy. Example, if 100 people visit your site and three people buy your product or service you have a conversion of 3%. And that's pretty good. The first thing to test is the headline and test the offer, and then test the price. Sometimes a higher price will outsell, a lower price, and sometimes a lower price will outsell a higher price. So the magic word is test if you're going to test price then start out with an extremely high price and work yourself down, because if you start out with a low price. Then the market might get mad and won't accept what you're doing. So start high and low, and always be tracking your conversion rate and do everything you can to increase by least 10%, 10% on the headline. 10% on the offer 10% on the price you may seem a compounds of your results.

Auto-responder is another great tool to invest in. The auto-responder allows you to automate the relationship building with your prospects. You can pre write messages, load, and have the messages go out to a set of intervals you decide. All done by e-mail. Messages sent out at a certain amount of time example. If someone signs up to your auto-responder that person will automatically get an e-mail and you can set up how long it takes to get the next e-mail. It can be from 0 to 10 days apart, or whatever you decide. E-mail is an excellent form of marketing because it doesn't cost anything to send an e-mail except your Internet access. Compared to a physical letter. If you send 1,000 letters, it's could cost up to $1-$4 for the package, and postage, which equals $1,000-$4,000. what if you send an e-mail it's going to cost zero e-mail can give you the power of repetition staying on the people's minds because as you've probably heard, out of sight out of mind. But with e-mails people remember you and if you've heard it takes a minimum of seven times contacts before, they will buy.

Every one of your customers and prospects should get a free e-zine/email from you, because like chapter before this one says, the more you are on a person's mind the more they buy from you, because you are trusted, and liked. Prospect doesn't buy right away. Eventually they will buy from you, even if it takes five years remember e-mail is free. And so keep on sending your e-zine/email, electronic newsletters to everyone, e-zine should be 65 characters long and hit the hard return, because not everyone's e-mail works the same and you can send out HTML e-mail, you can add your logo to it and make it look amazing. Send out emails, to test many different offers to see which one will be bringing you the most money

PayPal is the most popular website that collects money for you if you choose to accept their service. EBay owns PayPal, and if you want to be able to accept credit cards on your site. You don't want to spend any money on getting a merchant account. Then visit http://www.backseatbillions.com/recommends. If you want other sites that process credit cards go to google.com and type online processing. Like I said, if you don't accept credit cards, you are not in business because your average customer will use credit cards. Especially if you're selling a high-priced item $500 to $30,000 or more. PayPal have made it very affordable for the little guy to accept credit cards, because regular merchant account can charge you up to $700 to set up your account and $80 a month of service fees.

Delivering your product online can give the customer instant gratification at very high speed, an e-book is a book made into an electronic file. The most popular is the PDF file. E-books can go for all types of prices. Amazon has revolutionized the electronic book business with the Kindle. I'll let you know how you can capitalize on that platform. Another product you can deliver is an MP3 file and a video file. Can you imagine all the products you can turn into an electronic file? You can send and sell music, movies, looks audio books, home study courses online. The possibilities are endless. If you sell a physical product, like vitamins try to send an electronic product to satisfy them, because we live in an instant society: microwaves, fast food, fast everything and to stay up to the trned. Try to give instant gratification to your customers.

Ads placed in other e-zines can be a good place to test your products or an affiliate product. If you have an electronic product, you can go to www.clickbank.com and sign up with them and let them handle your affiliates for a small fraction of the profits and affiliate is a person that has signed up to sell your product and only gets a percentage of the sales price only when they sell it. You can have thousands of people promoting your products for pennies on the dollar, because people only get paid when they sell it. Another place to test your affiliate program is to use pay per click ads and banner ads. Yes, you can manage your affiliate program yourself it's going to eat up most of your time. And I mean a lot of time if you have thousands of checks to sent out. That's going to take up a lot of your valuable time that can be used to brainstorm other profitable ideas, hire this process out.

Delivering of your electronic product should be automatic, along with collecting the money and depositing the money in the bank. Automate your online business from the beginning because if you don't you'll get to the point. When you'll be so busy doing the work that you won't have any time to think and implement new projects. You should automate the collecting of money, if you use paypal they will do all of it. And also automate e-mails when people have questions that only you can answer. I have like a generic e-mail that says. Thank you for your e-mail. Please give us 48 hours to respond. Thank you, and respond to the nearly 48 hours people will be very impressed and think that you took the time to send them the first e-mail. So automate everything.

CHAPTER 11. Direct Response

Look at great sales copy (sales letters or messages) save the sales copy that makes you spend your own money. The only way to get good at writing direct response letters is to get the best sales letters and write them out by hand, soon you'll be able to write and know what's happening to make the person want to send money for your products. The most important function in any organization is to be able to get money. Whatever person knows how to persuade others to give money, will make a fortune. Copywriters can charge $5000, $50,000 even up to $1,000,000 dollars for a campaign, and keep 1% to 5% or more for royalties. Once I heard a copywriter say that he had to practice in front of a mirror to be able to hold a serious face when quoting the price of $25,000.

Solutions to problems is what you should be selling. Whatever you come up with has to do one of the following things: save time, money and or make them feel loved, respected, pleasure, relief from pain, make more money. Your product must be in one of those categories. People don't want just to spend money on automatic. You must get them to part with their money because they feel you have the solution to their problems. Back in the day. It was said that it's salesmanship in print. Now with the Internet, it says it's salesmanship online. Remember, human psychology has never changed, and ads that have been created century ago, can be adapted to do the same job, and that's to get people to give you money again, always be practicing the art of salesmanship, online, offline, in person, over the phone. Ect.

Headline is the most important component of a sales letter, it is said that 80 to 90% of what makes a sales letter work is the headline. The next thing to look is your offer, and you must ask for the money. Tell people what to do. Have your credit card handy, pick up the phone and dial 1-800 and order my product, or click on the buy button now. People have to be told what to do. Not only do you have rules for off-line sales letters but also for online sales letter on websites. If you come across a website that gets you to buy, or a physical sales letter, then study what was the process of how you were convinced to give your hard earned money. Some sales letters don't have to be super perfect to get the money. If you have a group of people that badly want, what you have, that's half the battle to get the money. Sell to people that want to buy. Soon you'll be super rich.

Color of the order form will affect your orders (conversion rate). The best color for the order for is goldenrod (yellow, mixed with orange), another component to have on your order form is the 1-800 order number and it has to run 24 hours 7 days a week. The order form must stand out on its own. It must have a great headline, present the offer in the first person and ask for the money. The sales letter is next best thing to a live salesperson, and the order form is an important part of this process. As time goes on. You'll learn from results, and you'll learn from other people's efforts. Do invent in books, home study courses, go to seminars, hire consults. To help you have a fulfilling business life. No matter what I or others say to you, it come down to you testing, to see what works for you.

Write down at least 50 of the best benefits your product give a person that buys it. Out of the 50, or so, pick the best benefit, and make it the headline for your sales letter, your website, your business card, your brochure, or on anything you want to attract people's attention. Again the headline is the most important part of the sales letter. The most basic form of headline stars with "How To" headline. You can start your headline, also with a question. Who else wants to _____? You can collect old ads from the 1930s, 1940s, and 1950s add them for your own use. An example of the classic headline. They all laughed when I said I wanted to play the piano. But when this headline has been adapted into many different headlines, like: they all laugh when I said I wanted to start my own business.

When I showed them my $2,000 check for one hour... Always be looking out for ads, you can adapt to use on your own.

Sequence your sales letter. First you have the headline, then you have the sub headline. Write out all of you headline ideas on 3x5 cards. Go through the cards, and pick the best headline out of the headlines cards. Remember the headline grabbes the reader's attention and make them read the subhead, and so on and on. If you need some help on making headlines, than visit http://www.backseatbillions.com/recommends and use the free software to make great headlines.

Short sentences should be used in your headline, about seven words, or less. All your paragraph should be short. If it's long, make a new paragraph. Your sales message. When being read, should flow if a person stumbles past a word change it. the way to see if it's following. Just get someone to read out loud your sales letter. Don't use complicated words used simple short words. The right level you should write for is third-grade level. No matter how smart a person is, they still like things to be easy to read, this way you get the people that don't have a large vocabulary. If you make it confusing for the person to buy, the first thing they say is no, that only stops the selling process. Short, clear, and simple to understand is what you want.

Relationship building is what you want to do with a prospect, because people buy from people they like and trust. The way to get them to trust you is to simply do what you say, and give them a free report. You can also give them at free sample, or an audit report. It should help the person. And if it had been something that helps them, than automatically you will build trust. The person that gets something for free will want to reciprocate. When a person buys you a cup of coffee, don't you feel obligated to buy the next couple of coffee for the person that bought you one. The free gift you give is doing a few things it's building your credibility, trust, and building a relationship.

CHAPTER 12. Money Make Money

Invest the extra surplus of money from your company. Also, give it to charity, about 10% 20% or more. You'll see that you make so much more money. When you start to give. Find and look for processes, people and strategies to cut your taxes. (I'm not a CPA, but if you need one, then get one). It's recommended that you higher a tax attorney to take care of your accounting. Because if your company ever got audited by the IRS. Your attorney will protect you, if he or she is doing the books as opposed to a CPA. If you get audited, the IRS can and will ask any questions, and the CPA will cooperate 200%, to help them get you in trouble. Also with the extra surplus of money, you can buy other companies. You can grow your company, and just be creative with what you can do with the extra cash.

Diversify your investment options. Study what and where you want to invest. Make it grow, if you let it sit in the bank, than the bank is making big money with your money. The best thing to do is to be your own investment broker, don't let someone else invest your money. The best manager of your money or your companies' money is you, now, if you don't have the power yet, just be patient, you will. Don't be afraid to take chances with money, because ultimately you can write it off, if the investment doesn't pan out. Before you invest, listen to what the experts are saying and make your own conclusion about things. The investments I recommend are: tax-free municipal bonds, zero-coupon bonds, high grade corporate bonds, and reits. You decide what you feel comfortable with. Some people have a high tolerance of risk taking, some people don't. No matter what you feel...invest the money.

Interest, and compound interest is the most powerful force in the universe of creating wealth. It won't take long to turn $1.00 dollar into a million dollars at 10%. Every dollar is a seed, a money tree seed. Respect the money you have and it will respect you. Money, remember, is just a tool, use it wisely. Be looking and planning to put your money into higher and higher, and larger yields. This way you can make the most money in the least amount of time. There's plenty of resources and books on where to invest to get the most amount of money in return. Ultimately the best one of the better way to grow the money is to start another company, or be the backer in a new company. If you invest your money as a partner, than expect to make 20% or more. Also you can buy companies that need to be fixed up, and sell it when you have turned it around, that's what Warren Buffet has done.

Benefits to staring a non-profit company can help you a lot. If you don't know anything about non-profit companies, just pick up a book on the library or at the book store on non-profit organization. Some of the benefits of running a non-profit is you can apply for grants, you can get people to work for free, called volunteers, you can have a great tax break, just because it's called a non-profit, but that doesn't mean that it doesn't make money. When you start your charity company, make it a non-profit. Give back to the community, this is a great plan. You can start your non-profit on a thousand different causes. Pick the cause that you are most passionate about. Because you and I were put on this earth to help humanity, and to contribute to the whole of mankind. It's recommend that you let a professional set up your non-profit organization.

Consistent behavior is an important trait to look for in a person that you want to give money to. If you want to be an angel, a financial angel, to grow the money, yes, there's a lot to look at, and to consider before investing. The best people you can invest with are people that are good marketers and sells people. If Dan Kennedy came up to me and said "Ronny, I want to start a limousine company, and I need $10,000,000.00 dollars" I would give it to him. In a minute, because as you know a person that can make people pay attention to your marketing, and cause a person to beg "Please, take my money!"

is a good investment. Another person to invest in is a salesperson, because no matter what business you create it's all about the marketing and sales working together for the greater outcome. You can take a calculated risk with these people, because even if they don't know everything that they need to know they at least know someone with the skills to help them.

High risk takers are much energized people. They make the most amount of money, and they learn the fastest, because they try more things quickly even if it fails, they just move on, until a project works. You might know a high risk taker. They move fast, are demanding, get it done right now, type of people. It's recommended that you read autobiographies of successful people. You will learn a ton, and because the more you know the better decisions you'll make. It's pretty amazing what you can learn from an autobiography. There's also the medium risk taker, accumulated wealth at a slower rate, than the high risk taker. Medium risk takers analyses carefully and make a decision they are 60 to 70% accurate on their investment deals. Than theirs the low risk takers, you know what they look like, you know what they drive. You know how they act. And their bank accounts are low on cash. With this said, you must choose your path, high risk taker, medium risk taker, or low risk taker.

Attorneys are a necessity in business and

especially if you are looking to do a leverage buyout. What is an LBO, if you don't know? You use the company's own asset to finance the purchase. The book recommended to learn about LBO is "how to do a leverage buyout" by J. Terrence Greve this is a genius of a book to learn from to expand your organization, you must learn to do LBOS. Basically, you're going to need people to trust you. People like investment bankers, people with large amounts of money or people that control large amounts of money. Willing to help you acquire the company you want. Nowadays you can sell low grade corporate bonds called junk bonds that are not collateralized by your company. This is an amazing tool to use even though the rate of return is high. The very smart about LBO be surrounded with people that know how to use this tool. Use this in your arsenal of tools get rich quick (very rich).

Commercial and residential real estate use to be a safe investment to do make. You still can invest in real estate, just be careful. Commercial property can make you large amounts of money. If you've never done real estate, then start out small with residential homes. A good course is by Carlton Sheets, called the no money down system. If you want to go to www.google.com and type in his name and see what site you can go to your. Another great person, you can learn from residential property to commercial property is Ron Legrand. And you can go and visit www.Globalpublishinginc.com the safest place to invest in real estate is the United States. If you want to invest in real estate outside the country be very careful and do your homework, because in some countries real estate value doesn't go up at all if it doesn't goes up slowly.

Trade and use only successful stockbrokers, and that they are investing his or her money. Once you get good. You can invest on your own. In the beginning, your trust on a broker that's playing with their money in the market, because there's plenty of young inexperienced stockbrokers trying to give you advise. You want to use a person that had been trading, and that has proven track record. Stop, remember, anything with large returns is risky. Just think, what type of person you are. You should be a risk taker, but a calculated risk taker, think like this. How much risk capital you have to invest to make the return. You want to make. If you're going to use $5000 to make $75,000, and the risk is minimal, but the rewards are high, so think how much risk verses, how much reward in return.

Ask your broker, what type of municipal bonds are available. Asked the broker to get you bonds that will mature 10 to 30 years out, or longer. The longer maturity day the cheaper it is to buy. Research what your broker tells you on the munis. You can sometimes substitute the munis with cash. Example, if you needed to borrow money and have no collateral. What you can do is borrow twice as much and with half the money buy municipal bonds to cover the entire loan and only pay interest. Example borrow $200,000 use $100,000 to do business. The other hundred thousand to buy municipal bonds, about 10 to 15 years out, that will mature to $200,000, and only make the interest payment. This idea works with private lenders, and not banks.

Maturity date is important when you're considering zero coupon bonds. This is another great way to grow your money. Ask your broker to look up zero coupon bonds. The longer the maturity date, the cheaper it is to buy in the present. You can do real estate deals, with zero coupon bonds. Example, if the house was worth $200,000, and no mortgage. You can borrow one hundred thousand, make sure the seller agrees. Then he'll get his money in about 10 to 20 years or longer. You can use $20,000 as a down payment to the seller, and with the remaining $80,000 by zero coupon bonds that mature to be $200,000. And you get the house. Not only can you buy real estate with the bonds, but also businesses be looking and thinking how to grow your money or the money, you're responsible for. It's a good idea to analyze all possibilities to grow your money.

CHAPTER 13 Your Upper Hand

Different techniques can be used to influence companies as well as people to get to think your way. The technique we're going to talk about is on intimidation. This technique is effective, but not recommend. It's sad that people respect violence, this technique should be used, very, very little. You want people to respect you and fear you in a non-action taking part from you. Some people will be intimidated by you, no matter what you do, and no matter how nice you are if someone respects you, because of fear. Don't waste your time trying to convince them that you are a good guy. Besides, if they respect you, because of it, don't change what they think, because this can be an upper hand for you. Do avoid any type of violence. If people are intimidated by how you look, that's good. People can be intimidated, just by how you talk, being respected, because the fear, is not a bad thing.

Energy is always moving and taking form from one form to another. It's a proven fact. Energy is not created or wasted. It just transmutes from one form to the other. Another motivator is the energy that comes from revenge. Revenge can be good or bad, it all depends what you do with that energy. If you want to physically hurt another person. That's not good, but if you use the energy to be better, at what you do, then you just won. Here's a story, a great CEO and president was and is the number one casino business owner. He'd been in business for about 25 years. The last hotel he created, he overspent by $400 million, and all the shareholders wanted to fire him. So, what he did was just cash in his shares. That was worth about $900 million, with the revenge energy. He took his money and build a better more spectacular hotel and casino. What he did was to take customers away from the people that try to fire him. Use the energy of revenge in a positive way to do your bidding.

Fast aggressive energy can come when you get angry. Again, you can use this energy in a positive way, or negative, but whatever you do, no matter how angry you get, restraining yourself from using violence, because we in the USA have a humane obligation to others not to harm anyone. If we were in another country, they use violence at as an everyday thing. When you get angry about something. It's a good time to ask yourself, what's good about the situation? If you say nothing and ask, what could be good about the situation? And answer the question. Anger can be transmuted from bad into good. It's also a good motivator. It all depends on your style. To get angry a lot, that it's time to switch professions, because if you get angry too many times. You can get ulcers and other problems that will affect your health. Anger is good, but not recommended because it can kill you sooner.

Negative energy can be created if you believe in superstition. If you've ever done any type of voodoo, you must stop. You think it's helping you, but it will hurt you. Once in my life. I didn't believe in black magic, until one person I know. She wished bad things to happen to a group of people, and all kinds of negative things were happening. And after that I was pretty shocked. My advise to you is don't wish to hurt other people, in any way shape or form. Even if they deserve it, because the law of karma will affect you whatever you do, and do to others will come back to you 10 times as worse, or 10 times as good, depending what you wished for on them. Superstition can help you, or it can hurt you, depends what you think. What you think and what you have experienced. If you believe in lucky rabbit's paw than by all means keep one. If you believe walking under a ladder is bad luck, than don't do it, because if you believe, it becomes a self-fulfilling prophecy.

Good energy exists, and you felt it. A lot people don't look at, or are they overlook is bad energy, and also exists. If you encounter bad energy. It's best to meditate and visualize you being surrounded by a big ball of white, positive energy, and you are at the center of the ball of white light. Make the white ball of energy bigger in all directions above your head below your feet all around you and see the white light push the black negative energy away from. You do this every day, and you'll see, that it makes a difference how your day goes. You should think of the ball of white positive energy as a force field around your body this way all day long you'll be protected. Even though this book is about business. All these techniques will give you a slight edge, because scientists don't know everything about the mind. Another way to deal with negative energy is to pray to the higher power to cast away the negative energies. And it's always good to pray and meditate.

Imagination can help you deal with the demons you have in your life. Evening like bad habits, anything that hurts your personal growth, you can to use your imagination, at its best learn to relax and imagine your demons dying or fading away and do this on a daily bases. In the morning, and especially before you go to sleep. If you are addicted to any chemical, do go to a detox center, look in the phone book, for detox centers. You don't have to be addicted to hard drugs. You can be addicted to regular pain medicines or over-the-counter stuff. Any type of drug will affect you and your performance. Don't let this demon rule your life, because it can ruin your life. Always be in control of the things you like, and the things you like to do, and don't let it become an addiction. If you drink, drink in moderation, or quit. If you smoke, just quit. If you need help, get it.

Chances are if you're reading this book. You have pretty good morals. It's vital not to do anything illegal that will affect your freedom being and doing illegal activities come with pretty big consequences. If you know of a person or people that are committing crimes don't associate with them, because you could find yourself in a whole lot of trouble, by association. Even if you didn't do anything illegal. I'm not talking about ex-felons. I'm talking about a person that's doing illegal things. In the preceding pages. I'm going to talk about ex-felons. Not all ex-felons are bad. So in this section, don't do anything illegal, on purpose, if you do something illegal, and you didn't know if it was illegal. You'll still be charged with a crime, and if you do business outside the US. Make sure you know the laws, because something you do in the US is legal, while in another country it might be illegal.

Defending yourself and stopping physical harm to another person should be the only time you use violence. If you are and in fear for your life, and can't run away, use any means necessary to protect yourself, and others. Other than those situations don't use violence. Even if you want to make a point. I know I speak from experience. No one likes violence, but everyone is capable of violence. Not only is it not good, but later, you feel bad. If you shot a guy, because he pointed a gun at you, and you were afraid for your life, and the other guy dies. You'll have to get counseling to deal with the traumatic experience. Never use violence on an employee that's not working the way you want them too. The only violence, you can use is the paper and pen. Just write them up, but never use physical violence on any person unless you are finding yourself or your loved ones.

Attitude is what you should look at when hiring an ex-felon. If that person has a bad attitude. Don't hire them, you know not all ex-felons are bad. Some actually learned their lesson. An advantage when hiring an ex-felon is that you can get a tax credit from the IRS. Ask your attorney, accountant about it. Another thing to look at is if the person is drug free. Plenty of people commit crimes because of drugs. People on drugs, whether their ex-felons and or not shouldn't be your project. Another benefit of hiring an ex-felon is the government will pay half of their wages. If you give seven dollars and the government will give another seven dollars so it's pretty good deal. If you can get an employee at half-price. Give people a chance, you might find a diamond in the rough, because if you're an ex-felon, you'll do better than the average person because it's already difficult to get a job, so he or she will do a great job.

Help people you love to stop using drugs if they use it. Remember people on drugs will lie to you, even if you are a good person. Be on the lookout of a loved one on drugs, because they will steal and lie to you. If you are patient and really love them help them once or twice to get them to stop, what if a are not willing to stop and don't want help. Then you must separate yourself from their presence. Don't let any person bring you down. Even if you love them. Just to let you go. Did you know that 50% of the cocaine produced in the world is consumed by the United States of America. Please don't be one of those people. The reason people use drugs is because they don't know how to change their state of mind. If you want to learn how to change your state of mind without drugs, then pick up a book on NLP (Nero linguistic programming) a good one is by Anthony Robbins called Awaken the Giant Within. Get it.

Loyalty is an import trait to have. If you know of people that cheat on their spouses, be very careful when you do business with them, because if this person can hurt a person they love, and was willing to marry, then watch out because they don't love you, they might like you, but just imagine how they'll treat you in business, very bad. Don't ever cheat on your spouse, just talk it over, and if you are not happy. Then get a divorce even, if you don't have a prenuptial agreement. You should just look for someone else to be happy with Staying in a relationship, you don't want will affect your whole life, including your business, and like I said, don't cheat because you will be judged not only on that, but the person getting the divorce can be awarded more than half of your assets. So, be loyal and faithful to your spouse and business partners.

Trust people until they do otherwise. If a person back stabs you confront them. Once, and just disown them. Forget them, and just don't talk with them anymore. You can even sue a person that talked bad about you. If people have been loyal to you, and if they have hurt you. Just forget them. So you can have a peace of mind. You don't have to associate yourself with them, no matter who they are. You should live your life to the fullest, and don't let anyone interrupt your peace of mind, your joy, your passion. Just get rid of them. People do a lot of evil things to you, but just stay away. This advice sounds something your parents say when you were a child and you know, what they are right. And always forgive and let go of people that hurt you. So that you can live your life to the fullest.

Eyes tell you everything about a person. What you hear is true. Just look at a person's eyes, and see where their eyes move. When you ask them a question, and you should know the correct answer. And if they answer correctly watch where their eyes look at, and when you ask a question that they can lie to you about, pay attention to where their eyes go. If their eyes are looking in a different direction than the one in the way their eyes were when you ask the correct question. There's a high probability that the person is lying. Another indication is the tone of voice. If they start to blink faster than usually, or blink slower than usual, if they do hand movements out of the norm for them. If they say words like "to tell you the truth" or "to be frank". If this person doesn't use those words often and decide to use these words. Look out, they could be lying to you. It's vital to know if people are lying to you. These techniques are used by the FBI, and other government agencies, and now you know.

Suspicious of people and companies. It's time to hire a private investigator. You'll be pretty surprised at all what you can find out about another person or a company. Spying on others is not bad. By spying, you can have an upper hand. You can do things better, by spying, you can protect yourself. It's not recommending you do the spying, but an outside professional company. You don't have to spy on everyone. The government already does that. Just spy on people. You think can hurt you, along with companies that can hurt you. I like to call it preventive maintenance. Fix it before it breaks. I'm not saying spying is good or bad. Use it to your advantage, use it to your benefit. The only thing I don't recommend is spying to get an advantage with stocks, it insider trading, because that can be called illegal and you could get a large fine and go to prison. If you're doing business with somebody you don't know, than have them investigated.

Lesson to learn is learn when to sue people and companies. This tool is a good advantage to use. When you reach the top and others are not good to you, sue them. If people or companies don't perform, sue them. It's okay to sue people and companies. If you were at the top and the company fires you, and doesn't want to pay what you've earned. Then sue them. If you don't have an attorney. Just ask other people, what attorney is good use. Keep in mind that this legal process can take a lot of time. And if you don't have the right agreement with your attorney. It can cost you a lot of money just too be able to use this tool. Only sue people and companies, that given you the short end of the stick on purpose. It's okay to sue. Don't feel bad. It's just another business tool to have on your side.

CHAPTER 14. Your Body

Forgive yourself and love yourself. It's critical, what you say to yourself. You can be your own biggest critic. DON'T. Just like yourself. You'll do much better in life. Take action to pamper yourself, especially when you complete a difficult project or when you feel like a break. Give yourself an enjoyable activity. Use loving words when talking to yourself. Never call yourself stupid, dumb, forgetful, clumsy, because like the saying goes. You are what you think. Instead use language that will empower you such as I'm a very successful person. I love myself abundance comes to me easily, I'm a tycoon. These are life, affirmations. Whatever you think of the most will affect your subconscious, and you'll be what you think about yourself. So always be loving yourself so that you can be able to love others.

Everyone judges the cover of the book, so it's important to be well dressed and have good hygiene. This will influence others, and command respect. If you look clean and smell clean, not only will you feel good about yourself, but people will treat you better. Try what I'm talking about. Have you ever been around a person that smelled? Not so good. You don't want to be around them, and you didn't care what they said, because you were focused on how they smelled. Have you ever been approached by a person that wasn't clean. What did you think, they are homeless? Don't waste your time. They're going to ask me for a handout. If you don't want others to think bad about you, what you want is people to respect you and follow you, so be a clean and well-dressed person.

Smart and loving are a few positive thoughts, you should think about yourself. A good positive self-image of yourself is important to your success. In anything you do, if you have a poor self-image. It will show, if you have a positive self-image. It will show. You want to think of yourself as a powerful, respected, resourceful person, because that is what will show. People will pick up on the energy and automatically give you that respect. If you don't want a position of power, then just think of yourself as a good, happy person. Be visualizing what you are, and what you want to be, but visualize, in the present and as if you already are what you want to be. Be careful when you think about the most, because it tends to happen. So be thinking, what you want at all times.

Workout to feel good about yourself. Not only does it make you fit, but it also raises your self-esteem. Looking clean and dressing as a successful executive will, and does raise your self-esteem. If you do business. Your self-esteem has to be up there. If you are not in

123

executive yet, dress as a successful one, because your self-esteem and self-confidence will attract the people to help you move up the ladder, and if you starting your own company. It's also vital to dress successful, talk successful, and act successful. Anything to help you along your path of success.

Self-esteem building should be on your mind. Yes, these few pages have been talking about self-esteem. Do things that make you feel good? A study says. When you laugh and feel good, your brain releases endorphins into your blood system. It's vital to feel good about what you do, so this way you'll always be growing. Growth is part of success, your success will grow along with your income. In the beginning of the year, plan fun activities throughout the year, for you to do. And then plan all business activities, this way you'll be looking forward to the year. And this keeps you motivated. Never lose your motivation. Guard with your life. Because if you lose your motivation. You'll lose everything. So do things that make you feel good and happy?

Bedtime should be a routine. If you sleep at 11 PM be consistent. When you are comfortable, and almost falling asleep. Think of one good thing you did, for that day, or think about what you learned. If you did do a good thing, and if you didn't learn one thing, the next day get up to catch up, pick up a book and learn something new, and if you can do at least one good deed, do it. So when you go to bed you will think of the one good thing you did that day. This will make you feel good, and build your self-esteem. Bed time is an important part of your day, because your subconscious mind can be easily influenced, and it's important to be thinking, thoughts that will empower you. Because it will affect your life.

Endorphins can also be released into your blood system, when you listen to music you enjoy. Music you like, will make you feel good. Music can make you feel sad and bad. Have you ever broken up and started to listen to a song that reminded you of the person you left, and all of a sudden you start to cry. Well, you see how it will affect you. Music can also help you think, it's always good to fill your car up with Mozart. You can also listen to baroque music. Music will give you extra energy. Music can also influence what you think. If you listen to negative words, you must stop listening to this music. If you pay attention to the lyrics of many songs, most likely, it's negative. You cannot afford to be influenced with negative thoughts. Listen only to good music with positive lyrics.

Different people have different skills. So don't compare yourself to others. Only compare yourself to yourself. Improve your skills, and don't try to be something you're not. Keep pace with yourself. If you make $100,000 year don't compare yourself with the guy that's earning $10 million a year. This can hurt your self-esteem, not to mention discourag you. It's a good idea to compare every 30 days where you are standing on your improvements. Before you are able to run a company, rather it's yours or not, you must work on yourself, because if you don't have the competence to run it, then you won't do great. The secret to anything starts with your thoughts, whatever your focus on becomes your reality. It's a good idea to see yourself succeeding.

Imperfect qualities we all have them, don't worship other people. Not only will this make you lose respect, but you'll be worshiping someone that doesn't deserve to be worshiped. Had you ever heard or seen people go crazy, or pass out when they see their favorite movie star or rock star. Don't let it get out of hand for you. Don't worship anyone or anything, only worship. The energy that's inside of you. If you believe in God, then that's good, because the energy that made you belongs to the higher power or whatever you want to call it. Remember, people can learn what you know, you can learn what others know, but more important. You know that you can hire people with skills. You don't. Never worship people only worship your divine self and God.

Gestures, a person makes can tell you a lot about them. It's a good idea to pay attention to a person's body position, body language, and what words a person uses. You can tell, what a person will do by just observing the few things. If you are interviewing a person, or are meeting a business prospect to do business with. It's a good idea to learn to read people, like a book. Take that skill, and surround yourself with people with greater skills, and skills that they do really well. It's like the sixth sense that they have. You can learn the skills of tiger Woods, but you won't play like him, because of the sixth sense factor involved. These are the type of people you want working for you.

Future relationships will and can be affected on how you treat people, especially if you don't know them, and they are affiliated with future prospect of yours, it's very important to treat everyone with respect and kindness. If the person is disrespecting you, just get away, don't insult them or say something too negative, because business no matter how big or small is all about people. Like I said, you need people to work for you and people to buy from you. The people you meet in the present affect your future, so it's very important to watch what you say, and what you do around people, because you never know, who they know. And it's good karma to treat everyone right. Treat others like you want to be treated, no matter how high or how low on the food chain ladder, they are.

Karma is a dangerous thing that can help you or

it can hurt you. The carrying of everyone, treat everyone right, because it will come back to you. And you'll feel good about it. If I was to ask you, you know of anyone that deserves something bad happen to them? And you did. You'll see karma working in the present, so be on the defensive side and always know what goes around comes around, sooner or later. If you hurt too many people your life will be a hard one to live. Too many bad things will happen to you. So be kind and caring to others, because you never know what's coming your way. Live and the care for others, most of the time, you'll understand.

Nonjudgmental is how you should listen to people, truly be interested in what they have to say, even if you're not particularly fond of the subject. If you ask questions about a person's interest just listen, you will be called the best conversationalist in the world. If you can't think of anything to ask, just remember this acronym HELP = H stands for hobbies example what are your hobbies? E stands for education, example where did you go to school? What certificates do you have? L stands for library, example what books are you reading? What was your favorite book? P stands for people ask who you know. What's your favorite celebrity? Who do you want to meet? Who do you admire? Just a little reminder just be a good listener and people will love you.

Lots of friends can be exhilarating, but you don't need lots of friends. You should have a few, at least one good friend, besides your spouse. Having friends is good for you, even if you get married, your partner can't fulfill all your needs. If you are miserable in your married life, then get a friend, and encourage your spouse to have friends, and you two should have friends. They serve a psychological purpose, because there's some things you can tell your spouse and then there's things you can't, but by having friends you can talk about anything. Friends can make you laugh, and you can have a good time. When you're feeling lonely, just call your friend.

Clothes you wear will affect people's reactions of you. If you want people to respect you, wear dark colors with a splash of red. If you want people to be fun and take it easy attitude, than wear light colors for example yellows, greens. The color combination, if you want to be respected, is black with some red, or dark blue, with some red. Another thing that will affect people, is how you speak, and the words you tend to use. Your attitude will also affect people. If you want to control people, then you must have a serious attitude, and every now and then, have a laugh, what if you start to laugh too much and made jokes, then people won't take you as serious. Remember the only thing you truly have is your reputation. If you want total control call people by their last names and have them refer you by your last name as well.

CHAPTER 15 Multiplying You

Age of a person affects what they can do, and know how to do. Not all people are equal. Some people have better talents, because of their background, and desires. You should treat people equals if that was the case we would all be making the same amount of income and we would pretty much have the same car, house, and etc. But that's not the case. You treat some employees better than others, because of what they can do, and what they know. The more they do, the more money you pay them. The more productive, hence better compensation. So when it comes to managing and delegating what to do with your employees, keep in mind their backgrounds and what they've done in the past, desires, and the older, the more experiences they have been through. The younger the more naïve they are remember, not everyone is equal.

Studies have confirmed attractive people have it much easier in life, then unattractive people. So for business, it suggested that you hire attractive people. It says that attractive people might do better because of their genes, genetic makeup. You can tell how a person will act just by how attractive they are. To see what I mean, higher attractive people, and see how others treat them. Look at most companies they send attractive women to sell you, it's better for business. Chris rock the comedian says" if you are attractive, life's going to be a breeze, but if you're ugly you're going to have to work real hard."

More things can be delegated if you have amazing employees, smart people or more productive and they cost less to train, because they remember the first time around. In the long run you can interchange them into different capacity and departments. Smart people can do other things for you, they can give you free time, more bang for the buck. Smart people work faster than not so smart people. You can't teach someone to be a fast thinker, they either are or they're not. Thinking fast can make a whole lot of difference. If you haven't experienced it, watch out, dumb people can cost you a fortune. Not all smart people want to start their own businesses, so you can exploit their talents for your benefits. Always be on the lookout for smart people. Smart people are not easy to spot.

Action is what needs to be done, and it comes only from go-getters. People that have that self-motivation are interchangeable between positions, because they are motivated to learn new skills, activities. You don't want to be a babysitter, your time, energy, and focus should be on growing your business, and to do that you will need go-getters. Not people that are lazy, dumb, and unskilled. These people take too much time to deal with. The best thing I can tell you is to develop a system to hire only go-getters, and is going to take trial and error to come up with a system. The way you build systems is not to be afraid to fail. Because you are looking for the correct sequence and to find it is by trial and error. If you want you can start using someone else's system defined go-getters for your company. Once you have that basic system you can make your own system.

Image is an important part of self-esteem, and for things to be done you need people with ambition and high self-esteem. It takes again, too much time for you to fix people that have low self-esteem. Self-esteem affects productivity. If your worker has low self-esteem he or she won't be as productive as they should, or worse, they'll get hurt on the job. You know what? Hire people with high self-esteem. These people affect other people, just at the opposite will affect the people, if you have an employee with low self-esteem. Get rid of them. Only hire good-looking, smart, high self-esteem people, to take care of your company, and yes there is an exception, if he or she is very skilled and you need their skill then hire them, but they must have high self-esteem.

Energy and your brain are all affected by your health, what you eat, and what you think. You and, the people you hire, have to have a workout program. Being physically fit, your body affects your thoughts, if you are working on a long project, it's going to be stressful. Period if you're unfit it will be hard for you to finish and will affect your profits. So to over come these negative affects you must work out every day, and you must alternate with weights one day, and cardio the next date and take one day off from working out. Your competition is in better physical shape, then he will be smarter and faster than you. If nothing else you should be at the same physical fitness as your competition so you can have the opportunity to take over the market.

Fear is one of the many tools to use to manage people. You can hire aggressive people to manage others, because they get things done. If you put a person that is weak in a position of power, then he or she will be a weak link in your organization. Hire people, that have a backbone, they will get results you want, and give them positions of power, and I know aggressive people get things done, and yes you might have to get the aggressive manager to tone it down a bit, but from what I've experienced aggressive people get it done and they are worth it. If you don't like that, then you don't have to hire aggressive people, test this idea for yourself. If they are too aggressive don't worry just take advantage of them.

Hire happy people, they are more productive, because they can deal with more stress. You get more, from an optimist person. You have to test everything I talk about, don't just take my word for it. If you hire a pessimistic person then you're going to get, why it won't work, if you hire an

133

optimistic person they say, why it will work, and you should have both types on your staff to see who has a better reason to move forward, or not. This is a sneaky trick to have these two types of personalities on your staff and remember ultimately it's your decision to move forward with the project or not.

Time, money, and profits are affected when you hire good people. Good people are hard to find. What do I mean by good people? Employees that show up on time, work very hard and smart. That don't do drugs, doesn't drink. Maybe in the future when they come up with a cure for drug addiction and alcoholics, and when that happens then maybe you can hire very skilled ex-alcoholics, and drug addicts. Now let's stay focused on good people that make profit at least three times what you paid them. If you are paying $50,000 a year they must be producing $150,000 of work for you, if they don't you must pay them less. Only pay more when they do more and not just because they have been in your company for 50 years. Only pay on value produced.

Frustrated is what you get if you hire dummies, not to mention all the time and money wasted. What I mean by dummy. A person that doesn't have natural skills, like memory, not able to effectively see what needs to be done. You know what dummy when you see one. Again you don't have the time, money, and patients, it will be wasted on dummies. Focus your energy on high energy ambitious natural intelligence people. I guess what I'm talking about is a person with RAM like RAM from a computer the bigger the RAM the faster your computer works, and because you can piece the human together you must look for the natural intelligent people, because once you've downloaded knowledge into them you don't have to do it again.

Problems risk and headaches will be your reward for hiring people with low self-esteem. I know I told you before, and I will tell you again. These people are not your problem. Their problems can't be yours. and you're not the one to fix these people's problems. You only have so much time and so much energy, and so much resources to accomplish your objectives and people will be a big part of the puzzle, but people that don't need any fixing. Besides you're not qualified to be a psychiatrist, only focus your resources on profits keep that in mind. Profits people and projects that make the most money. A lot of money truckloads of money.

Frustration and loss of productivity and loss of money will be your reward if you hire lazy people. Yes, another negative trait you don't want to associate yourself with. I know you are smart. How do I know? You're reading this book, and I bet this is not the only book you're reading about success. Lazy people are like the plague to productive people. You don't want to affect your hard-working employees with the lazy ones. If that happens you might as well fire everyone that's affected. Once laziness has been made into a habit, it's hard for people to break it, and again not your job to fix "it" the only way to find out if someone is lazy is to hire them and just observe what they do or what they don't do and make your decision, to keep them, or not.

Profits can also be affected by passive people, so don't hire them. Theirs three types of people: 1 people that make it happen. 2 people that watch what happens. 3 and people that ask what happened? If you would have to put passive people in the category it would be in the third type category. Passive people are another form of laziness. Stay away from them, unfortunately the only way to find out is to higher and observe, then decide to fire them. This chapter is a little negative, but to have positive results you must know negative results. Good and bad, rich and poor, profits and loss everything as an opposite side sometimes it's okay to have both, the balance things out, but being passive, lazy, dumb, evil etc. etc. are not qualities you want or want to balance out. Stick to the positive characteristics of people.

Balance must be achieved in your empire, that's why I recommend you hire people that are pessimistic to see how your project can fail, and take steps to stop it from failing. Higher optimistic people they will tell you how to get positive results while pessimistic people will tell you why you'll fail. You just have to be smart enough to have a systems for your projects and your decisions. One thing to keep in mind, it's okay to get negative results as long as you adjust and keep adjusting until you get the results you are looking for. So hire pessimistic as well as optimistic people. One coin has two sides to it. Why not take advantage of it. Be smart and use this idea.

Employees are sensitive to people that are evil in nature. People that are evil should not be higher in your empire. Evil people can be dangerous and can even cause death, worse - loss of profits...Ha! Ha! Ha! I know bad joke, but you get my drift. Don't hire people that are mad at the world, because anything can set them off like a firecracker. Evil people are easy to spot. You can also feel the anger and madness. Don't do business with evil people. Protect your life and profits.

CHAPTER 16 The Rich & Powerful

"Positive thinking won't guarantee success, but negative thinking will guarantee failure."
                                                  Ronny
Engelke

Money, power, wealth, love, and respect is all for the taking. And it's up to you to make it happen, and it's up to you to decide to make it. Everything you want in life, regardless of what it is, it starts in the mind first your mind is basically the powerhouse where everything comes from. If you don't have in your mind first you won't have in your life. Every single idea you've ever had in your life and that has manifested in your life started in your mind first.

Your mind is like a projector, and the light of the projector is your energy. The film is your thoughts. Whatever you think about the most (the film) will project on the canvas of your life. If you have a piece of film with negative scenes on it, it's going to project on the canvas of your life. If you have a piece of film with positive scenes on it it's going to project on the canvas of your life. It is vital to only run positive scenes on it all the time. Positive thinking.

Another way to put it. Your mind is like a

garden, you have one little seed of thought, and it grows into a huge tree. Some thoughts take longer to come true, and some thoughts manifest very quickly. And here's what you have to pay attention it doesn't matter what kind of seed you plant in your mind, it's going to grow. So it's vital to have a seed of positive outcomes. What I'm saying is only think about the things that you want to come true, but make sure it's the positive things in your life. Because if you think about a negative, any negativity will come true for you. Example if you think to yourself I don't want any bills, more bills is what you're going to get. Because you are thinking about bills. Instead you should think I am making a ton of money. You have to think in a positive because with everything about will come true in your life.

The way that I was able to work with many billionaires, is quite interesting. I few years ago a friend let me borrow, more like pushed me to listen to an audio album by Anthony Robbins called Unlimited Power, and than I discovered a book called Awaken the Giant Within, by the same author. In this book there was a section where you had to write down, and read six sentences. The questions went something like: What are you happy about? Or What could you be happy about? Who do you love? Who loves you?, and a few more questions. I don't know what got into me, but I decide to write one more extra sentence, "I'm a billionaire" I wrote that

139

phrase on a 3x5 card, and taped it to the mirror in the bathroom, I taped another in my car.

Your not going to believe what I'm about to tell you. I started working for another limo company. While working at this new company, within 14 months of reading every day "I'm a billionaire" I drove the first billionaire. I didn't even know that he was a billionaire.

An executive had requested a town car, he sat in the front next to me. While he was on the phone, he indicated to the person on the other end to give him the phone number, but I didn't see him pull out a pen. So while driving at 70 mph. I pulled out a pen and paper, and gave it to him. I was just giving customer service. I didn't know that my gesture of pulling out a pen and paper. Would cause him to request me every time he came to Las Vegas. The next week, I'm reading the Forbes magazine, the 400 wealthiest people on earth. I was fantasizing, I scratched out Bill Gate name as the riches person, and put my name there. While flipping the pages, I saw the picture of the guy I drove. He was worth $900,000,000.00 dollars, he was the CEO of DreamWorks, Jeffrey Katzenberg. Mr. Katzenberg, not knowing to him that I chose him to be my mentor. I learned so much from him. What I realized was that a person can become a billionaire. The Forbes magazine is off on the true number of people's wealth. If Mr. Katzenberg would sell all of the shares owned by him, and indirectly, by him. He would be worth many billions of dollars. I'm super grateful to have had the chance to work with him. I wish Mr. & Mrs. Katzenberg the best.

By working with Mr. Katzenberg, I was able to build my reputation. Pretty soon, I was working with Steven Spielberg, David Geffen founders of DreamWorks, Larry Ellison founder of Oracle, Paul McCartney from the Beatles, Bob Iger CEO of Disney, Barry Meyer CEO of Warner Bros., Kevin Tsujihara the New CEO of Warner Bros., Meg Whitmen CEO of HP, Tony Hsieh CEO of Zappos.com,   Scott & Cyan Banister internet investors, Donald Trump real estate mogul, Jerry Bruckheimer award winning film producer, Tom Cruise award winning actor, Leonardo DiCaprio award winning actor, Keanu Reeves award winning actor, Jamie Fox award winning actor. David Foster award winner music producer. Mark Burnett. Lionel Richie award winning singer, Rod Stewart,

I also have worked with Lady Gaga, Justin Bieber, Usher, P Diddy, Jennifer Lopez, Jennerfer Gardner, Sandra Bullock,   Steve Harvey, Cedric The Entertainer, Jerry Lewis award winning entertainer, Mariah Carey, The Kardashian Family, Paris Hilton, Nicky Hilton, Ellen DeGeneres, Dead Mouse, Afro Jack, Avicii, Steve Aoki, Holly Madison, Pasqual Rotela, Toby Maguire, Christopher Walkin, Silvester Stalone, Sugar Ray Lenord, Mark

Walberg, Donni Walberg, N sync, Back street boys, Randy Jackson, Tim McCraw, Faith Hill, Jonah Hill, Tyrese Gigson, Luis Miguel Latin America singer, Steven King, Mel Gibson, Selena Gomez, and the list goes on, and on.

I am not bragging to you by letting you know who I've worked with, but to let you know that these are all people like you, they overcame some things in life, but not all. You too can accomplish so much in your life, if you apply yourself. Stop over thinking so much and apply yourself.

Decide what you want to accomplish, and do it. I know that sounds easy, but doing it doesn't. the only thing stopping you is fear.

Fear can mean "**F**ace **E**verything **A**nd **R**ise" or "**F**inding **E**xcuses **A**nd **R**easons" whichever one you choose is true for you. Choose correctly. If you have fear, and it's not allowing you to accomplish your goal, than ignore the feeling of fear, If you are nervous, before giving a speech, just ignore the feeling, and do it anyways. To get a better understanding watch this video online https://youtu.be/u4YaaQVGwFg

Remember you are your reality. Your are your own creation. Create wisely.

Get Your Free Video Training

visit: http://www.backseatbillions.com/training